The Yankee Pioneers

(Frontispiece). Alone in the wilderness.

Samuel B. Pettengill

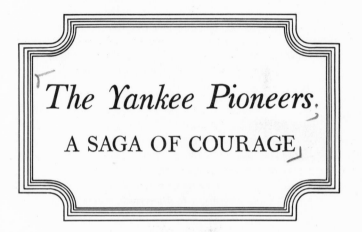

The Yankee Pioneers,

A SAGA OF COURAGE

CHARLES E. TUTTLE COMPANY
Rutland, Vermont

Representatives

Continental Europe: BOXERBOOKS, INC., *Zurich*
British Isles: PRENTICE-HALL INTERNATIONAL, INC., *London*
Australasia: PAUL FLESCH & CO., PTY. LTD., *Melbourne*
Canada: M. G. HURTIG, LTD., *Edmonton*

Published by the Charles E. Tuttle Company, Inc.
of Rutland, Vermont & Tokyo, Japan
with editorial offices at
Suido 1-chome, 2-6, Bunkyo-ku, Tokyo

Copyright in Japan, 1971
by Charles E. Tuttle Co., Inc.

Library of Congress Catalog Card No. 73-158785
International Standard Book No. 0-8048-0981-x

First printing, 1971
Second printing, 1972

PRINTED IN JAPAN

Dedicated to my dear wife
Helen
without whose constant help
during seven years
this book would not have been possible

Table of Contents

Table of Contents

List of Illustrations

Preface

I HAVE SPOKEN before audiences in forty-four states. In introducing me the chairman has generally said that I had been brought up in Vermont, and that my ancestors had lived there and in New Hampshire and Massachusetts since about 1640 when the first Pettengill came to Salem from England. When the meeting broke up it was almost certain that some persons in the audience would come up to shake my hand and say with pride that they, too, traced back to New England. This convinced me that people still admire the sheer courage and grit of the brave men and women who conquered the New England wilderness. (This is, of course, equally true of those who settled all of the other wilderness states from the Atlantic seaboard to the Pacific.)

This book was written as a tribute to one of those pioneers, my great-grandfather Peter, who was born in New Hampshire before the American Revolution. In 1787, when he was eighteen years old, he walked over a hundred miles at the shoulders of a team of oxen to

11

settle in what was then a wilderness and become a citizen of Vermont.

I have attempted to incorporate in this book as much detail about the daily lives of such pioneers as I have been able to find. So much of what went on in those early days was taken for granted that little was written about it, and today what was once common knowledge has been largely forgotten. For instance, when the pioneers first came to the wilderness there was no grass. When I read this in an old diary I was amazed until I walked through the woods near my home and found—no grass.

This made me wonder what else happened that we do not think about today. And the idea of this book was born—to gather all the bits and pieces of information I could find and put them together to make a picture of how our pioneer ancestors lived when they first came to the wilderness. It is the story, not of just one man or one family, but of many who settled in different parts of New England. Despite different problems, all these men and families had one common denominator—courage to face up to their problems.

It is important to remember that with the exception of the power of gun powder and that of river water harnessed in mill dams, the immense task of settling the wilderness was done by only the muscle power of men, women, children, oxen and horses. Steam engines did not come into use in America until after 1800. Decades were to pass before gasoline, fuel oil, natural gas and electricity did all the hard work of the American people. (It has been estimated that the average factory worker today does only about one per cent of the total "work" in making his product.)

It would make too long a list to name all the books, records, diaries, letters and other documents I read over a period of more than five years to collect my facts. So at this point I want to thank all the men and women, living and dead, whose writings have been of such great help to me in ferreting out the past.

Eight of the illustrations in the book were selected from a collection of historical drawings owned by the National Life Insurance Co., of Vermont, who generously gave me permission to use them. Drawn from studies of Vermont history by two artists, the late Roy F. Heinrich and the late Herbert Morton Stoops, they show costumes, episodes and backgrounds in accurate accord with the past.

The log cabin in the woods (Frontispiece) was photographed by Michael W. Munley and first appeared in the *Times-Reporter* of Springfield, Vermont. It portrays graphically the loneliness of a pioneer cabin in the forest, and I am grateful for their permission to reproduce it.

Maurice and Virginia Sanders of Wintersville, Ohio, have for some years been spending their vacations making rubbings of gravestones in old New England cemeteries, preserving from the elements and vandalism what has become a lost art. (In fact, the carving found on old gravestones is considered to be the earliest form of American folk art.) In an old cemetery in my home town of Grafton, Vermont, there is a stone memorializing a mother, young son and thirteen infants buried together. The epitaph is quoted in many gravestone anthologies and is famous for the sad story it tells. The Sanderses made a rubbing of this stone to illustrate my chapter, "Death and Burial," and grateful acknowledgment is made to them. The original rubbing can be seen in the Museum of the Grafton Historical Society.

SAMUEL B. PETTENGILL

Happy is the man who recalls his ancestors with pride, who treasures the story of their greatness, tells the tales of their heroic lives, and with joy too full for speech, realizes that fate has linked him with a race of goodly men.

—GOETHE

[1]

The Untold Story

For fifteen thousand years or more the red men had been the only inhabitants of New England. Then in the early 1600s the white men came. Scores of books have been written about the old days in Yankee-land when it was settled by the white men. But for the most part the details of daily living in the first years of bitter struggle with the wilderness have been omitted, or buried in an avalanche of words concerning the military, political, economic and ecclesiastical events and wars of two centuries. Important as they are, the average reader finds plowing through them too long and dreary a task.

This tale is confined to the plain people of Vermont and New Hampshire, and other New England states, as they did their hard work and faced hunger, disease and death, often alone. It is further limited roughly to the first quarter century or so in the wilderness. It should be noted that this twenty-five year period varies from town to town as they were settled in different years. The more southern towns had a thousand people or more when townships to the north had only one or two pioneer families.

To illustrate: When Vermont's first census was taken in 1791, just before it was admitted to the Union as the fourteenth state, not one of what later became fifty-six towns had a single inhabitant. The entire territory of what is now Orleans County had only thirty-seven people. Each of forty-seven other townships had less than one hundred people. Similar figures could be given for all the New England states.

Whatever the date of its beginning, when a settlement had enough people to require a saw mill, a grist mill, a general store, a blacksmith shop, a school, a church, a resident physician and a post office in a corner of the village store, it was no longer pioneer country. Most of the books on colonial life and the household arts and crafts deal with already settled communities.

Thus confined in time and terms of years, I do not know of any other book that concentrates on the first few years before a community had gathered; when it was one man or one family, or two or three or a dozen families in the wilderness, often with no neighbors within ten, twenty, or thirty miles.

Written contemporaneous records of these early years are very scarce. There were plenty of goose and crow quills, but steel pens were not invented in England until 1803, and at first cost two to three dollars each. Graphite and clay pencils, somewhat similar to those used today, were first invented in France in 1795, but neither steel pens nor pencils came into general use much before 1830. Writing paper was extremely scarce, partly because England imposed a heavy tax on paper entering the colonies, just as she had done on tea. It was inevitable that the early pioneers left very few diaries, journals, letters or first hand, on-the-spot records of their first grim struggle with the wilderness.

The untold story is: what they were up against.

This story should be made available to our generation. For if the Yankee pioneers had flinched from their hardships, returned home, or had gone to softer climes, New England would have lost the priceless ingredient of grit and character of which this present age is in great need.

As Vermont's historian, Zadock Thompson, wrote in 1842, "They were aroused to their highest energies by the difficulties they were compelled to encounter."

As they reshaped the wilderness, it shaped them, and to a large extent our country.

[2]

Yankee Blood

Yankee blood flows in the veins of millions of Americans. Have you ever wished to know more about the way the first pioneers lived and how they faced the challenge of a new raw land? Let us then go back in imagination to the first years spent in the wilderness of New England.

What did the endless forest have to say to those ancestors of ours? And with what voice did it speak?

Imagine a one-room cabin at the edge of a deep forest. The nearest neighbors are one, five, or more miles away. It is night and there is no moon. Winter is approaching and the whispering of the first white flakes can be heard. Some of the flakes are drifting in through cracks in the roof. The big trees are swaying and crackling in a rising wind.

The pioneer family whose name you perhaps bear is sitting around the fireplace. They gather strength from its warmth but as the flames rise and fall, the shadows of father, mother and children change their shapes in strange ways on the walls around them. The fire is their only light. An old dog mutters and growls in his sleep.

But these are not the only voices. Waking from its daytime sleep, an owl hoots. Although he is known to be harmless, the hoot has an ominous sound. Not far off, a bear barks. He weighs perhaps four hundred and fifty pounds.

Further away, a pack of wolves begin to howl. They are hungry, always hungry. In the crotch of a nearby tree, a coon begins to wail. Then comes the scream of a panther.

Little is said. The father banks the fire with infinite care to make sure, very sure, that it will rekindle when daylight comes. It will be cold in the cabin at daybreak. The water in the bucket will be frozen. As the fireplace embers die down, the room grows dark.

[3]

Great-Grandfather

I have often wished I could go back in time, say to 1800 or thereabouts, and spend a year with my great-grandfather, Peter Pettengill. And then return to this 20th century, remembering all I had seen and heard.

What a tale I could tell! Researchers and historians from far and wide would flock to my door. Boys and girls would clamor for me to "tell us about the old days." As I did so, their elders would gather 'round and one of them would say, "My great-aunt Comfort told my mother that the pioneers made their first candles out of the wax found in bee trees. And that before their young apple trees bore fruit, they made vinegar out of maple sap." And so on, for hours on end.

On this visit to the past, I would wish to have an invisible camera with a mile of film, and a voice recorder to catch the old Shakespearian pronunciation and roll of words now obsolete, but which I once heard used by an old hill-country friend. I would wish also to know all I know now about the 20th century, but not tell anyone what I knew or that I was Peter's great-grandson.

I grew up in the same small township which he helped to settle. As a small boy I fished for minnows and dace in the same brook where he could easily catch a big mess of trout; I made hay in the same fields where he once swung a scythe; drove a team of oxen just as he had done; pinched potato bugs to death; slept as he had done on a rope bed in the north bedchamber (the coldest room in the house). In summer I slept on two corn husk mattresses, and in winter between the two. The only heat in the house was the kitchen stove; to save work the fireplaces were seldom used, usually only when we had company. In bitter winter weather the fire in the kitchen stove would go out and the water in the kettle would turn to ice which had to be thawed in the dawn's early light in order to prime the pump in the corner of the room.

In summer's blinding heat at haying time I mopped my brow in the shade of a great elm that was familiar to great-grandfather as his eighty-eight summers came and went. And in late winter, when cold nights but warmer days caused the sap to run in the "sugar bush," I helped collect the thin sweet liquid from the wooden buckets we had earlier hung on the maple trees after tapping them and inserting wooden spouts. It took forty gallons of sap to make one gallon of syrup then, just as it does now, and still more boiling down to make maple sugar. But the results were worth the effort. Is there anything better than maple syrup on hot pancakes on a cold winter morning?

Great-grandfather came to Grafton, Vermont, from the little town of Salem, New Hampshire in 1787 when he was eighteen years old. He must have walked the entire distance of over a hundred miles, as he drove a team of oxen which needed someone at their shoulders to guide them with "gee" and "haw" unless they were on a familiar road.

Born seven years before Lexington and Concord Bridge, and the son of a Revolutionary soldier, he could also tell much about the generation before him.

His new home was still in wilderness country. As proof, Keene, New Hampshire, only thirty miles away and a much larger town than Grafton, voted in 1782 to pay a bounty of forty shillings a head for killing wolves which were making it a heart-breaking job to raise sheep. In 1789, within a few rods of Keene's main street, the wolves did kill several sheep. And in the nearby town of Westmoreland, in 1788, a man was surrounded by seven wolves, but "receiving immediate assistance, he escaped their devouring jaws."

One of Peter's uncles, James Pettengill, was one of the first three settlers at Peabody Point, now Gilead, Maine, where he was killed by Indians in 1781. This was only six years before Peter came to Grafton.

Over the door to the Farmers' Museum at Cooperstown, New York, are these words: "Show how the plain people of yesterday, in doing their daily work, built a great nation where only a great forest stood."

How could the first pioneers manage without matches, butter, vitamins, rubber footwear, bathtubs, electric milking machines, gasoline powered saws, horseless

Gathering the maple sap.

wagons, R.F.D., telephones, super-markets, beauty shops, television, hospitals, drug stores, sleeping pills, headache remedies and electric tooth brushes?

And did the "young-uns" feel abused because they had to sleep on corn husk mattresses and help with the chores?

[4]

The Two New Englands

In 1620 and for a century or so thereafter, the territory that is now New England had two major characteristics, the sea and the forest. It may be said that from the standpoint of making a living, there were two New Englands.

The sea, of course, was first. The settlers from Europe came by the sea and on its western shore they made their first explorations and settlements. The ocean was a highway that required no construction, no bridges, no tunnels. It had no hills to climb, no rivers to cross, no snow to be removed. It was then and now the cheapest of all thoroughfares for the movement of people and commerce. Travelers on the sea were free from Indian attacks.

New England was settled from the sea and the early settlers lived close to it and by it. For their food and livelihood they depended chiefly on the sea: building, outfitting and repairing ships, deep sea fishing, shell fishing, whaling, sealing, the evaporation of salt water to produce salt, the making of lime from clam shells and imports to and from the Old World, the West Indies, the East Indies and faraway China.

New Bedford, Massachusetts, and Sag Harbor on Long Island, New York, were the great whaling towns. Of Stonington, Connecticut, an old-time record says that "in some years one hundred thousand seal skins have been brought to this place."

This is all symbolized by the "Sacred Cod" that hangs in the State House in Boston and is the official emblem of the state of Massachusetts. Seacoast New England lived on and off the sea.

There was of course no fixed boundary, then or now, between sea and forest. Some big trees grew close to the ocean's shore. Generally, however, the strips of low-lying seashore swept by tides and high winds had few of the giant trees such as were found inland in Maine, New Hampshire and Vermont.

Beyond the coast country was the "great forest." It is not possible for the present generation to visualize its immense sweep and height. The forest was thousands of years old and covered New England, especially the northern part, like a dark blanket. Because the red men had neither axe nor saw, nor anything of iron, they had hardly touched it.

Living today in homes heated by fuel oil, natural gas, coal and electricity, it is almost impossible for our generation to really grasp the size of the great forest trees and their service to man. Here were thousands of square miles of fuel for warmth against bitter cold, for cooking food and washing clothes. Here was the timber with

28

which to build the ships that sailed the seven seas, and also build log cabins, furniture, barns, fences, bridges, baskets, churches, cradles and coffins. Here, too, was food, including at least five kinds of edible nuts. Here were sugar and syrup. Here was wood for the handles of hammers, axes, forks, shovels, saws, the beam of plows, the snath of scythes; here was the material to build ox-yokes, ox carts, the wheels to harness the power of water falls, to make children's toys or the tiny works of a wooden clock, the pegs to serve in place of nails. Here too was potash, turpentine, rosin, dyes and the material for scores of other uses. As late as 1800, wood supplied ninety-four per cent of all the energy, other than muscle, wind and sunlight, that was used in the United States.

The prime tools for forest land were the axe to cut and the plow to plant as soon as the axe had done its work.

The forest and the man-created clearings in it called for lumbermen and farmers, far different callings from those of the men and women who chiefly lived by, on and from the sea.

To paint one clear picture of the difference between the forest and the sea, Portsmouth, New Hampshire, on an arm of the ocean, was settled in 1653 and in a generation became a city with fine houses and buildings for commerce and manufacturing. A century went by before white men settled in what became Salisbury, New Hampshire, only forty-nine miles north and west as the crow flies from Portsmouth. In 1756, Daniel Webster's father and three or four other pioneers settled in Salisbury. Mr. Webster is reported to have said that "no other white man could be found north of his log cabin until he reached the St. Lawrence River in Canada."

Because the great forest of New England has been much less reported to our generation than the ocean and the settlers on its shores, this narrative is chiefly centered on the forest and the farming that followed when trees were cut and the sun shone through.

I record a number of instances of hardship and struggle, failure and success, naming places and persons. Most of these relate to Vermont and New Hampshire towns, because their old-time records and books are more accessible to me. Similar instances can no doubt be found in all of the New England states.

[5]

The Pilgrims' First Winter

The white man's first permanent and best known settlement in New England was, of course, that of the Pilgrims at Plymouth, Massachusetts, in 1620.

Because the Mayflower left England very late in the
fall and was over two months at sea, it is probable that
the Pilgrims, as a whole, suffered greater hardship during their first winter than any other settlers on the New
England coast. It was the first settlement to include a
large number of women and children. Two babies were
born on the voyage, one a still birth.

This is highlighted by one stark fact—half of the
Pilgrims died during their first year! Aside from the
anguish that death brought to the survivors, they had to
dig graves in frozen ground without visible markers for
fear that Indians might see them and violate the graves.
The consolation that a headstone provides to perpetuate
the memory of the dead was denied to the living.

Fortunately there was small trouble from the few

Indians who had survived a frightful pestilence only a couple of years before.

The Pilgrims made their first landing on November 21, 1620 (old style) at what is now Provincetown at the tip of Cape Cod. They then spent four weeks exploring the coast for the best place to settle. It was not until December 22 that they decided on Plymouth. Winter was then upon them.

Thousands of Americans visit Plymouth every year. They see the reconstruction of the pioneer village known as "Plimoth Plantation" as it was believed to be in 1627 or "seven years after the Pilgrims landed." The reconstruction is splendidly done with meticulous fidelity to the known facts.

It must not, however, be thought to portray the surroundings and miserable hovels of the Pilgrims during their first winter in 1621, or the second winter or the third. As Governor Bradford wrote in June, 1625, the Pilgrims "never felt the sweetness of the country 'till this year," four years after landing.

No one can begin to feel in his bones what the Pilgrims were actually up against that first cruel winter until he reads *Mourt's Relation, a Journal of the Pilgrims at Plymouth*, edited by Dwight B. Heath with ample footnotes. This journal seems to have been compiled by several of the Pilgrims. It was published in London in 1622.

Governor Bradford also wrote a *Diary of Occurrences* which was also published in 1622.

Consider their primal needs on landing: fresh water, food and fire. The crowded Mayflower which had been their shelter since leaving England on September 8, more than two months before, was completely out of wood to keep them and the crew warm and to cook their food. They had also to be kept supplied with fresh water. One of the reasons for deciding to settle at Plymouth was because there were "brooks of very sweet, fresh water running down to the sea."

Due to the shallowness of the harbor, the Mayflower had to be anchored about three quarters of a mile from the shore. "We were much hindered in lying so far off from the land."

Here it stayed until April 5, 1621, when it started its return to England. Contact with the land was made in the "shallop." This was a big rowboat with eight or ten oars and could also be fitted with a small mast and sail. It was probably about twenty feet long. It had been brought over on the deck of the Mayflower and had been so badly damaged that extensive repairs had to be made during the winter. Incidentally, the Mayflower had been so crowded by the Pilgrims and the ship's crew that a number of the men slept in the shallop on the deck during the crossing.

In the shallop a dozen men could go from ship to shore and back again when the waves were not too high. "The breaking waves dashed high" many times that winter. There was no wharf or dock on the shore to facilitate landing. This meant, of course, that some of the men had to jump into the cold water and pull the shallop onto the beach every time waves and tides made the trip possible. While the shallop may have landed many times at or near the famous Plymouth Rock, it is doubtful that many landings were made on its slippery surface without anyone getting wet.

As Mourt relates, "water froze on our 'cloths' and made them many times like coats of iron." They of course had no rubber boots or oilskins. (It was not until the 1870s that most of the difficulties involved in making rubber footwear, raincoats, etc., were overcome.) Soaking wet in freezing weather was the way some, or all of the men, started the day's work.

They made bonfires on the shore where they could warm their hands, but little more. There were no tight roofs anywhere. The men who did not get soaked landing the shallop were often drenched in freezing rain or covered with snow. In this condition, the men on land often worked all day in half-frozen footgear and clothes.

"John Goodman had his shoes cut off his feet that were so swelled with cold, and it was a long time ere he was able to go," i.e., to walk. Many of the men's deaths were attributed to this ordeal. "Some of the people who are dead took the original of their death" in their cold, wet shoes and clothing.

Great toil was required to "fetch our wood" even in dry weather. Trees had to be cut down, cut up and dragged to the beach by the strength of human backs alone. They had neither ox nor horse to help them. "Our greatest labor will be fetching our wood which is half or a quarter of a mile, but there is enough so far off."

Some of the trees were cut up and used on the shore for firewood and rough shelters. Among their tools, besides axes, the pioneers probably had an "up and down" or pit saw, operated by two men. This made it possible to saw tree trunks lengthwise to make planks and what they called "clap-boards."

The wives and children, and the sick persons on the Mayflower had to have warmth to stay alive, and cook their frugal meals of fish and flesh. It was four years before any of the Pilgrims, including their babies and small children, had any cow's milk! It was 1624 before three heifers and a bull were brought over from England. It is no wonder that they called the days and months "a pinching time."*

Added to their other woes, they were in debt. Their voyage had been financed by the "Merchant Adventurers" in Old England, and the Pilgrims had agreed to send back a shipload of lumber to England, which was very short of wood.

In addition to lumber, their contract bound them to send back dried or salted fish and furs, and to do so for seven years.

During that first winter "our greatest labor was the fetching of our wood" to apply to their contract, and to start "the building of our town."

From the first they started to build "ye house for common use," that is, a combined warehouse, tool room and fortress against possible Indian attack. As they did so, some men stayed on shore at night as well as day, and increasingly so as the winter months passed into spring. Women and children and the sick stayed on the ship until shelters were made on the shore.

To quote Governor Bradford's history and his spell-

* *Early History of New Hampshire*, by Rev. Henry White, 1841.

ing, "We clave faithfully together in ye maine. . . . Ther dyed sometimes two or three of a day . . . In ye time of most distres ther was six or seven sound persons . . . who fetched them wood, made them fires . . . and with abundance of toyle . . . made their beds, washed ther lothsome cloathes . . . did all ye homly and necessarie offices for them which quisie stomachs cannot endure to hear named."

On shore, "in frost and snow they were forced to make the earth their bed and the snow their covering." We have nothing to tell what their shelters were. They were probably huts of "wattle-and-daub," that is, sod laid over a framework of small saplings, bent over in the form of a cone, like Indian wigwams. Some caves may have been dug in the hillside.

Of the one hundred and two Pilgrims who left England there were twenty-eight wives and daughters. One boy baby, Peregrine White, was born on board the Mayflower and lived to the ripe old age of eighty-four years. This boy's father died during that first cruel winter. His mother married another Pilgrim, Edward Winslow, whose wife had also died during that same terrible time.

This was the first marriage ceremony in New England. Edward Winslow later became governor of the colony.

On April 5, 1621, the Mayflower started back to England, leaving behind the making of a nation.

[6]

The Endless Forest

In 1524, a century before Plymouth Rock, the great Italian explorer, Verrazano, after whom the huge bridge across New York harbor is named, sailed along the New England coast and "saw ill pleased the shadows and the gloom of mighty forests."

No one can begin to appreciate the gigantic task which confronted the pioneers unless he is able to visualize the endless and often impenetrable forest. Blot from your eyes the open vistas of today and try to see only what the pioneers saw "with the eyes of discovery."

Except in the northernmost counties of Maine, New Hampshire and Vermont, there are today few stretches of highway which are solidly bordered with trees on both sides of the road for more than four or five miles. In 1750 a pioneer could tramp from Massachusetts to Canada in practically unbroken forest.

There were of course a few vistas in the olden time, ponds, lakes, beaver swamps, granite hill tops with too little soil for trees to root in and "fire burns." In 1752 a fire burned for over fifty miles from the White Mountains to the Atlantic coast. Hurricanes or "blow downs" occasionally leveled a mountainside.

There were also a few square miles along river banks where Indians had girdled and killed trees with their stone axes and thus made a little space where corn and pumpkins could grow in the sunlight. Except for these bits of open land, it was a wilderness of trees. "The whole town [of Rockingham, Vermont] was an unbroken forest . . . the gloomy forest shaded the deep rich soil that the summer sun had not warmed for centuries, old decaying trees which had fallen in every conceivable direction among the living giants of the forest and the thick undergrowth formed an almost impenetrable barrier to travel."

It was in fact, the "forest primeval" that had covered the land since the end of the last glacial period, two hundred centuries ago. It was a place where men used few words and spoke very softy. Many eyes might be watching, many ears listening. And as birds sing in the sunlight but are hushed in the shade, it seems probable that the stillness of the great forest had something to do with the taciturnity of Yankee speech.

The forest primeval which "stood like Druids of eld" in Evangeline's time in Nova Scotia covered New England also like a green blanket. The wilderness was a part of the great forest which covered all of the northeast quarter of America from the Atlantic to the Mississippi River, the greatest continuous forest of the western hemisphere.

It was endless. America, east of the western plains country, was trees, oceans of trees. It has been well said that America could never have become what it is without the forest. In 1800 wood provided ninety-four per cent of the country's energy for heat, cooking, the building of homes, barns, fences, bridges and all the rest. As late as the Civil War, railroad locomotives burned wood.

It is an old saying that when the Pilgrims landed, a squirrel could go all the way from Plymouth Rock to the Mississippi River without touching ground, eating nuts as he leaped from one tree to the next.

It has been about twenty thousand years since the last Ice Age slowly began to retreat northward, draining Lake Champlain of its salt water and exposing the scarred New England rock and earth to the healing warmth of the sun. During the centuries that followed, trees had lived their natural life spans, died and lived again. It was virgin forest for five or ten times as long as the Christian era, now nearly two thousand years. There was nothing other than occasional fires or hurricanes to prevent trees from growing to their natural height and girth. Man and his axe had not arrived.

"There were giants in the earth in those days." In his history of Vermont, published in 1809, Samuel Williams gives the diameter and height "of the greatest trees which are to be found in most of our towns." Pines, he says, grow to six feet in diameter or about nineteen feet around, and up to two hundred and forty-seven feet in height. The greatest of the maples, elms, hemlocks, oaks and ash trees grow to be from one hundred to two hundred feet high. He tells of an elm in

Dunstable, New Hampshire, that was cut down in 1736, when George Washington was four years old, that had a diameter of seven feet, eight inches. This would give a circumference of about twenty-four feet.

Sanborne's *History of New Hampshire* reports that Eleazer Wheelock, who founded what is now Dartmouth College in 1769, said that trees grew two hundred feet high on the present campus, and "in one instance, by actual measurement, one tree was found to be two hundred and seventy feet long," which is about the height of a twenty-story building. These are the words of a clergyman and college president.

Not many church steeples in New England are much more than one hundred feet high. So when you go to church next Sunday, imagine that where the steeple now stands, a tree may have stood that was twice as high as the steeple.

Giants such as these were exceptional of course, as giants always are, but it seems probable that many such giants were living in most of New England, except perhaps along the seacoast, when the white men came. What a place for Paul Bunyan and his Blue Ox!

The trunks of these huge trees that grew near one of New England's great rivers were floated down to salt water to become ship masts so tall that some of them were one hundred and twenty feet above the deck.

An elm once stood in Connecticut that had a girth of thirty feet and three inches.* It was killed only a few years ago by the Dutch elm disease. A tamarack tree

* *The Great Forest*, by Richard Lillard, 1948.

once stood in Tamworth, New Hampshire, that was ninety feet tall.

The largest tree I know of in New England that is still standing is the "Lafayette Elm" at Kennebunk, Maine, under whose shade General Lafayette was entertained in 1825 when he paid his last visit to the land he loved and helped to liberate. This beautiful tree is a living monument to the days of Franklin, Washington, Jefferson, Adams, Hamilton, Ethan Allen and all the "men of '76." The tree is now nineteen feet, four inches in circumference, and is still growing. I am glad to report that a public-spirited family has given this magnificent tree to the town of Kennebunk with a trust fund to care for its needs.

It would be a splendid thing if the good people of every New England town were to locate their oldest tree and then protect it as a living historian of days long gone. School boys and girls would be a little prouder of their towns if this were done.

[7]

What? No Grass?

I remember well my surprise when I first read in a chronicle of the long ago that "only when the forest was chopped down did the grass come creeping, creeping everywhere, on the hillsides, in the valleys, by the brooks and around the cabin doors, covering the world with a delightful green, giving an attraction to the landscape that nothing else could."

It had never occurred to me that when the white men came, there was practically nothing that we would call grass today. The native grass did not grow in deep forest shade. The *New Hampshire Gazetteer* of 1823 says that "this state was originally an entire forest, both as to the mountainous regions and the plains and valleys." It does not mention the correlative fact of no grass.

If you would understand the struggle that confronted the first settlers you must realize the absence of grass. Few can grasp the significance. It is something the historians have missed. Stranger still, it was seldom mentioned in journals the pioneers left us. Probably the absence of grass was so obvious at that time that scarcely anyone saw any need to mention it.

As we gaze today on the broad meadows of New England, the open hillside pastures, highways, towns and villages with few trees, it takes an act of the will to see in the mind's eye what the first settlers saw, and what they did not see—grass.

Later on we shall see how for lack of grass (hay) Seth Hubbell's ox "gave out." He starved to death. Without oxen the pioneers were "pack animals," unable to plow, harrow or haul heavy loads.

There was some "wild grass" here and there, but its value as food for cattle was practically nil. "The native grasses of the uplands were rank, but innutritious so that settlers found it better to fodder their cattle on the salt herbage of the sea marshes."* But this of course could be done only by those pioneers who lived on or near the marshes.

Without grass or hay there could be no cows, milk, oxen, sheep or horses. The green leaf is a power plant for all living things, the mightiest converter of the sun's energy in the world. "Grass is the magic carpet upon which all humanity rides."

A cow needs to eat fifty or more pounds of grass or hay a day. A working ox needs to eat up to twice as much. If a pioneer attempted to get enough beaver marsh "hay" to keep a yoke of oxen or a cow all winter, he would have little time to gather firewood for himself.

On the sides of rivers where the sun could warm a bit

---

* Palfrey's *History of New England,* 1866.

of soil a few hours a day, or on the shores of ponds and lakes, or on the edge of wet beaver marshes where the beavers had gnawed down the trees, or along granite ridges on the hill tops, or where a forest fire, started perhaps by lightning, had killed square miles of trees, or where a hurricane's scythe had mowed them down, as in 1938, there were small patches of native wild grass. Seth Hubbell and the other pioneers called it "browse," a mixture of wild grass, leaves, twigs, sedge, ferns and small brush.

As an example, out of Vermont's nine thousand square miles of land area it is doubtful that there were more than a hundred, and maybe no more than fifty square miles of "browse" when the white men came. And "browse" is starvation food. It stays outdoors the year around, hence is either wet and mouldy, or dry and sere, having lost its nutrients.

As an old record puts it, "When they came to winter cows on inland hay, and feed upon some wild fother [fodder] as was never cut before, they could not hold out the winter . . . many of their Cattell [cattle] died, especially if they lacked Salt Marshes."

The wild native grasses of New England, in fact of all the United States, were very inferior stuff, even on the western prairies, either for grazing in the summer, or as hay or fodder in the winter. Practically all native grasses have long since been replaced by British and European grasses, one of which, cocksfoot or "orchard grass," was imported from Britain for the very reason that "it will grow in shade."

The absence of grass is further shown by a provision

in many of the "grants" in New Hampshire and Vermont that were made by Governor Benning Wentworth, requiring each grantee "to stock with English grass five acres of land within three years."

As every farmer knows, hay should be cut when grass is in flower, left in the sun only until it is nearly dry, and then put under cover and kept dry. The next time you are at a beaver marsh imagine yourself wading up to your middle in the wet swale with a sickle or scythe cutting wisps of wild grass, and "backing" them to a rude shelter or outdoor stack for your ox or cow next winter!

It is recorded that a poor woman, living alone on the seacoast of Maine, cut wild grass with a pair of scissors to keep her cow alive during the winter. The only part of New England where wild grass grew to any considerable extent was along the seacoast, where the shore was exposed to sunlight. Tides and onshore wet winds provided the necessary moisture; because the ocean never freezes, this narrow belt of land was warmer than inland areas.

It was along the seacoast also that the great bulk of New England Indians lived when the white men came. As they had neither cattle nor horses, the wild grass was of no importance to them as fodder, but it was useful to them for basket-weaving, mats, bedding and so forth, and of course the ocean was an unfailing supply of food: fish, clams and lobsters.

"But how about deer and moose? They lived in the wilderness forests for centuries without grassy meadows and pastures. Why couldn't cattle do the same?" One answer is that many deer do perish during the winter from cold and the lack of nourishing food. But most survive. All animals adjust to their environment or die. The Algonquin Indians' name for moose was "twig eater." Moose live on twigs, bark, lily pads, etc. Moose and deer are apt to kill young trees by gnawing off their bark for winter food. There are instances when starving pioneers themselves gnawed the bark of trees.

"But what about the Great Meadows that bordered on the Connecticut and other big rivers? Weren't they fields of grass?" When the white men came, they weren't meadows. They were woods and did not become meadows until they were cleared. The "Great Meadows" at Putney, Vermont, for example, were "originally covered with magnificent white pine" which became the first mast timber from Vermont for sailing ships. *The History of Eastern Vermont*, by Benjamin Hall, confirms this statement. "At Putney, the Great Meadows were not more than half cleared of their noble forest of yellow pine." Similar observations were made about Fort No. 4 at Charlestown, New Hampshire, which became a meadow only as the trees were cut.

The greatest obstacles that faced the pioneers were neither the Indians nor the cold winters. They were the "never ending forest" and the absence of grass, which meant the absence of ox power. In more than three hundred books on the pioneer period, I have found only one clear-cut statement of this basic fact. In *The Winooski*, the careful historian, Ralph Nading Hill, writes that the early settlers had only "the strength of their arms and backs between existence and extinction. They could not bring their animals because there was nothing in the woods for them to eat." Without their animals they could not bring their heavy tools such as grindstones and anvils, but only small tools such as axes and augers carried on their backs.

A soldier tramping through the wilderness of Bennington, Vermont, recorded in his journal that "there is no doubt when the timber is sufficiently killed and laid open to the influence of the sun and air, that it will yield good crops of grass and flax." This is one of the very few original pioneer statements to be found about the absence of grass in forest country.

By the word "killed" he probably meant "girdled." Girdling was done by chopping off the bark near the ground to the quick of the tree. This could be done in a few minutes. It killed the tree which was left standing. The following year the tree had no leaves. The sun could then reach the ground, and crops and grass could be grown in the patches of sunlight. Girdling saved time. It enabled a settler to farm much earlier than if the trees were all cut down, cut up and burned before planting his first crop, a time-consuming operation. Later the trees were cut down and used to build cabins, sheds and fences. Or they were burned as fuel or to make potash. It took years of Herculean labor to get rid of the stumps and roots.

The name of one of our favorite grasses, "timothy," comes from Timothy Hansen, born near Keene, New Hampshire, in 1707. He went to Europe and brought back the first "timothy" grass seed sown in America. He wanted a "croppe that he could sew [sow]." Other

47

kinds of European or English grass seed must have been imported in large quantities from an early date, for in 1755 a requisition for supplies to build a fort on the Kennebec River in Maine reads "there must be sent to Ft. Western 10 lodes of English hay, for the supply of ye oxen that must hall ye timber for ye building of Fort Halifax, other wise wee can not go on."

As stated in a semi-official history of Vermont in 1925, "The chief product of Vermont today is the grass in the pastures and hayfields which is converted into milk, butter, cheese and meat for market."* Botanically, "grass" includes wheat, oats, barley, rye, buckwheat and sunflowers as well as clover, alfalfa and timothy. These are the important grasses and of them it can be stated unequivocally that there were none in Yankee-land when the white men came.

If you call Indian corn a "grass" as a botanist might do, it constitutes a small exception to the general state-ment about the lack of grass. For example, there were the "Great Meadows" at what is now Newbury, Ver-mont, and Haverhill, New Hampshire. Here was a wide valley with ox-bow turns in the slow flowing Connecti-cut. There were probably less than three square miles of what we now call meadows in the ox-bow flats. From time to time, perhaps for centuries, wandering Indian tribes had developed on these flats some rudimentary agriculture such as Indian corn and pumpkins.

Either by girdling or by fire they had killed enough trees to clear about one thousand acres, less than two of

* *Vermont, Its History and Geography,* 1925.

48

the nine thousand square miles in Vermont. Some native grass must have come up with the corn and the pumpkins, but the Indians had no cattle or horses to feed it to.

The fact that the ox-bow flats induced the white men to struggle through sixty miles of forest wilderness to get to them from No. 4 at Charlestown, New Hampshire, and from Concord, still further away, is proof enough that there were no grass-covered meadows between them and Haverhill and Newbury.

As Vermont's first *Gazetteer*, published in 1824, says: "Our lowest meadow lands, or intervales, were formerly covered with oak, elm, butternut, etc. The higher flats were, in general, covered with pines." This is correct, except that it seems to imply that meadows and intervales are the same thing. They are not. A meadow is a piece of grassland whether used for raising hay or for summer pasture. An intervale is a low-lying tract of land along a river, in between hills, and does not become a meadow until it is cleared of trees.

In all the centuries before the white men came, what was there to prevent trees from growing on flat land as well as on hillsides, as they grow today? The forest takes over the meadows as easily as it does the hillsides. Every New Englander has seen this happen whenever a farm is abandoned.

In the 1700s there was a favorite "Forefathers' Song":

> The place where we live is a
> wilderness wood

Where grass is much lacking
  that's fruitful and good.
Our mountains and hills and
  the valleys below
Being commonly covered with
  ice and with snow.

[8]

A Soldier of the Revolution

Very few of the first settlers in New England left a
personal, detailed record of the hardships they endured.
Most of their stories have come down to us from their
children and grandchildren who told what their sires and
grandsires had told them. By that time it was legend,
accurate in broad outline, but no doubt often magnified
by family pride.

One who did leave such a record was Seth Hubbell,
who with his wife and small children settled in what is
now Wolcott, Lamoille County, Vermont, about thirty-
one miles from the Canadian line. He started his long
journey from Connecticut late in February, 1789. It is
apparent that he had spent the previous summer alone
in the wilderness, to start clearing and to begin a cabin.
He was then in the prime of life, thirty years old.

Seth Hubbell was with General Washington at Valley
Forge and continued in the service of his country to wit-
ness the surrender of Cornwallis at Yorktown in 1781.
He then lived in Norwalk, Connecticut, until he decided

to make a "pitch" in the new Republic of Vermont where he spent the rest of his life.

The first pioneers had little time for writing, nor did Hubbell for many years. Paper was very scarce. Pencils as we know them did not exist, and a goose quill pen and homemade ink were awkward tools in gnarled hands.

In 1824, when he was sixty-five years old, Seth Hubbell did write a narrative of the struggles and hardships he and his wife had endured. I quote: "He is sensitive of his inability to entertain the curious, but if his simple words can reach the sympathy of the feeling heart . . . it may serve to still the murmurings of those who are settling in a neighborhood of plenty . . . resulting from the toil of the few who broke the way into the wilderness."

His narrative which covers the first seventeen years of his residence in Vermont appears in Vol. II of Hemenway's *Vermont Gazetteer*. I have cut his narrative by considerably more than half, but assure the reader that the omitted incidents are as grim as those given here. Where he uses the word "backed" it means that he carried the load on his own back. Some of the mileages to the nearest settlements are my own computation as the crow flies.

The problem of his sick ox which "gave out" can be understood only by readers who know that it takes two oxen to balance each other on a yoke. It is probable, too, that Hubbell was poorer in tools and equipment than others who later became his neighbors. (Two years after he came, Wolcott had a population of thirty-two.) For

Helping the failing ox.

this reason he suffered more hardship than other pioneers with more oxen and tools. He wrote:

> In the latter part of February, 1789, I set out from the town of Norwalk, in Connecticut, on my journey for Wolcott, to commence a settlement and make that my residence; family consisting of my wife and five children, they all being girls, the eldest nine or ten years old. My team was a yoke of oxen and a horse. After I had proceeded on my journey to within one hundred miles of Wolcott, one of my oxen failed [became exhausted], but I however kept him yoked with the other till about noon each day; then took his end of the yoke myself and proceeded on in that manner with my load to about fourteen miles of my journey's end, when I could get the sick ox no further, and was forced to leave him with Thomas W. Connel, in Johnson; but he had neither hay nor grain for him. It was now about the 20th of March; the snow not far from four feet deep; no hay to be had for my team, and no way for them to subsist but by browse [twigs or brush]. As my sick ox at Connel's could not be kept on browse, I interceded with a man in Cambridge for a little hay to keep him alive, which I backed, a bundle at a time, five miles for about ten days, when the ox died. We still had eight miles to travel on snowshoes, by marked trails—no road being cut.
>
> Esq. Taylor, with his wife and two small children, who moved on with me, were the first fam-

ilies in Wolcott. To the east of us it was eighteen miles to inhabitants, and no road but marked trees.

I had now got to the end of my journey. I had not a mouthful of meat or kernel of grain for my family, nor had I a cent of money to buy with, or property that I could apply to that purpose. I however had the good luck to catch a sable. The skin I carried fifty miles, and exchanged for half a bushel of wheat and backed it home. . . .

We had now lived three weeks without bread; though in the time I had bought a moose of an Indian, and backed the meat five miles, which answered to subsist on. No grain or provision of any kind, of consequence, was to be had on the river Lamoille. I had to go into New Hampshire, sixty miles, for the little I had for my family till harvest. The three remaining children that I left in Hyde Park [distance nine miles], I brought, one at a time, on my back on snowshoes, as also the whole of my goods. . . .

I moved from Connecticut with the expectation of having fifty acres of land given me, but this I was disappointed of, and under the necessity of selling a yoke of oxen [apparently Hubbell had acquired an ox to take the place of the one that died] and a horse to buy the land I now live on, which reduced my stock to one cow, and this I had the misfortune to lose the next winter. That left me whole destitute of a single hoof of a creature, and the next summer I had to support my family without a cow.

In the fall I had the good fortune to purchase another cow, but my misfortunes still continued, for in the June following she was killed by a singular accident. Again I was left without a cow.

When I first came into Wolcott, my farming tools consisted of one axe and an old hoe. The first year I cleared about two acres, wholly without any team. When too faint to labor, for want of food, I used to take a fish from the river, broil it on the coals and eat it without bread or salt, and then to my work again. This was my common practice the first year till harvest. I could not get a single potato to plant the first season, so scarce was this article. I planted the land which I cleared in season with corn, and an early frost ruined the crop. My seed corn I had to go twenty miles after. . . .

My scanty supply of bread-corn made it necessary to improve the first fruits of harvest at Lake Champlain, to alleviate our distress. Accordingly on the last of July or the first of August, I took my sickle and set out for the Lake, a distance of better than forty miles. I was a fortnight on this tour. My wife was fearful some accident had happened. I left my family without bread or meal, and was welcomed home with tears. . . .

I had the good fortune to buy on trust of a man in Cambridge, twenty-four miles from home, twelve bushels of corn and one of wheat. I also procured twelve or thirteen bushels of potatoes. This grain and potatoes I carried on my back.

In the course of Divine Providence events do

take place out of the common course of nature, that our strongest reasoning cannot comprehend and is impious to deny. In fact a signal Providence seemed to direct the path for me to pursue to procure this grain. Though I was doomed to encounter perils, to suffer fatigue and toil, there was a way provided for me. . . . In the course of the winter I was so fortunate as to catch sable enough to pay the debt by the time it was due. I had now gone to the extent of my ability for bread-corn, but was destitute of meat. I had to have recourse to wild meat for a substitute and had the good luck to purchase a moose of a hunter; and the meat of two more I brought in on shares—had the one for bringing in the other. These two were uncommonly large, were judged to weigh seven hundred weight each. The meat of these three moose I brought in on my back, together with the large bones and heads. I backed them five or six miles over rough land, cut up by sharp ridges and deep hollows, and interspersed with underbrush and windfalls, which made it impracticable to pass with a hand sled, which could I have used, would have much eased my labor.

Those who are acquainted with this kind of burden may form an idea of the great difficulty of carrying a load on snowshoes in the time of a thaw. It is wearisome at such times to travel without a load; but with one, especially at this late season, it is intolerable, but thaw or freeze, my necessities obliged me to be at my task, and still to keep up my burthen. I had to draw my fire-wood through the winter on a hand sled; in fact, my snowshoes were constantly hung to my feet. . . .

Being destitute of a team for four or five years, and without farming tools, I had to labor under great embarrassments; my grain I toed in the three first years. After I raised a sufficiency for my family, I had to carry it twelve miles to mill on my back [to be ground into meal] for the three first years; this I had constantly to do once a week. My common load was one bushel, and generally carried it eight miles before I stopped to rest. My family necessities once obliged me to carry a moose hide thirty miles on my back, and sell it for a bushel of corn and bring that home in the same way. . . .

I was about out of meal, and had previously left a bushel at a deserted house about five miles on the way. A neighbor and I accordingly started before sunrise; the snow was light and we sunk deep into it. By the middle of the day it give some, which made it still worse; our snowshoes loaded at every step; we had to use nearly our whole strength to extricate the loaded snow. It seemed that our hip joints would be drawn from their sockets. We were soon worried—could go but a few steps without stopping; our fatigue and toil became almost insupportable—were obliged often to sit down and rest and were several times on the point of giving up the pursuit and stop for the night, but this must have been fatal, as we had no axe to cut wood for a fire; our blood was heated, and we must have chilled. We finally at about dusk reached the de-

serted house, but was in effect exhausted. It seemed
we could not have reached this house had it been
twenty rods further; so terrible is the toil to travel
through deep snow, that no one can have a sense of
it till taught by experience. We struck up a fire and
gathered some fuel that lay about the house, and
after we had recovered strength, I baked a cake of
my meal [probably on a hot stone]. We then lay
down on some hewn planks, and slept sound till
morning. . . .

I obtained knowledge of there being beaver on
a small stream in Hardwick, and desirous to improve every means in my power for the support of
my family, and to retrieve my circumstances, I determined on a tour to try my fortune at beaver
hunting. With difficulty we struck up a fire, but
our fuel was poor, chiefly green timber; the storm
increased; the snow continued moist; our bad ac-
commodations grew worse and worse; our fire was
not sufficient to warm us and much less to dry us;
we dared not attempt to lay down but continued on
our feet through the night, feeding our fire and
endeavoring to warm our shivering limbs. This is
a memorable night to me, the most distressing I
ever experienced.

We worried through the ten miles home at the
dusk of the evening, nearly exhausted by fatigue,
wet and cold, for it began to freeze in the morning;
our clothes were frozen stiff on our backs; when I
pulled off my greatcoat it was so stiff as to stand up
on the floor. In order to save our traps we had to

make another trip, and one solitary muskrat made up our compensation for this hunting tour. . . .

In the year 1806 we were visited with sickness that was uncommonly distressing, five being taken down at the same time, and several dangerously ill. In this sickness I lost my wife, the partner of my darkest days, who bore her share of our misfortunes with becoming fortitude. I also lost a daughter at the same time. . . . Though I have been doomed to hard fortune I have been blest with a numerous offspring; have had by my two wives seventeen children, thirteen of them daughters; have had forty-seven grandchildren and six great-grandchildren, making my posterity seventy souls. . . .

When I reflect on these past events, the fatigue and toil I had to encounter, the dark scenes I had to pass through, I am struck with wonder and astonishment at the fortitude and presence of mind that I then had to bear me up under them. Not once was I discouraged or disheartened. I did in reality experience the just proverb of the wise man, that "the sleep of the laboring man is sweet, whether he eat little or much." Nor can I close my tale of suffering without rendering my feeble tribute of thanks and praise to my benign Benefactor, who supplies the needy and relieves the distressed.

* * *

The undersigned, having read in manuscript the foregoing narrative, and having lived in habits of intimacy with, and in the neighborhood of Mr. Hubbell at the time of his sufferings, we are free to inform the public that we have no doubt but his statements are, in substance, correct. Many of the circumstances therein narrated we were at the time personally knowing to, and are sensible more might be added without exaggeration, in many instances wherein he suffered.

THOMAS TAYLOR, Justice of the Peace
DERIUS FITCH, J. of Peace
JOHN MCDANIEL, J. P.
JESSE WHITNEY, J. P.

Seth Hubbell died in 1832 at the age of seventy-three, leaving his "rich, beautiful farm to his sons."

Some readers may think that Hubbell was the victim of his own folly in starting his long journey in February. It is, however, probable that he wanted to start while there was still snow on the ground for his sled to run on, not realizing how much deeper the snow would become as he went north.

It was much easier to move heavy loads in winter on sleds, sledges or "stone boats." It was thus that the huge stones in the foundations of houses, barns, bridges and so forth were moved into place in the old days. Any pioneer could make a wooden sledge, whereas axles, spokes and iron-rimmed wheels called for experts. In fact, years later when there were roads of a sort, it was still the custom to move heavy loads on sleds, because wheeled vehicles would "bog down" in muddy ruts.

Many southern New Englanders were not familiar with Vermont, New Hampshire and Maine winters. Witness a college graduate who, with his family, came to Townshend, Vermont, ten years after Seth Hubbell's journey. They left Uxbridge, Massachusetts, on March 9, 1799, with their household goods mounted on a sled drawn by two yoke of oxen. When they left Uxbridge there were only three inches of snow.

When they reached West Townshend, the snow was six feet deep on the level and it took "nineteen yokes of oxen" of the neighbors to "break out" a road and drag the sled up a steep hill to their new home.

One of the family was a fourteen-year-old boy named Peter. It was his assignment to lead the family cow, on foot, the entire distance. As the crow flies, this was not less than ninety miles, and considerably more over hill and dale on foot. The last name of this boy was Taft. Had he lived until March 4, 1909, he would have been very proud to witness an event that took place in Washington, D.C., in which his grandson figured prominently.

While Seth Hubbell's struggle with the wilderness was very grim, it should be kept in mind that the first settlers in the other frontier towns of New England had similar hardships to endure.

[9]

Pack Animals

No one can really appreciate the iron courage of Seth Hubbell and hundreds like him unless he understands that the measure of courage is not alone the greatness of their difficulties, but the smallness of their means for meeting them. It is one thing to make a path through a wilderness with a bulldozer and a crew; another, to do it alone with only an axe.

This point is seldom made. When the Pilgrims landed at Plymouth Rock in 1620, there was not a single ox or horse in what is now New England. The Pilgrims had no "working cattle" or oxen.* In all North America there were no cattle when the continent was discovered. They were "first brought to the Western Hemisphere by Columbus in his second voyage in 1493." It was not until 1624 that three heifers and a bull were brought across the ocean to Plymouth. In short, the Pilgrims had no milk for four years! In 1630, ten years after the

* Palfrey's *History of New England*, 1866.

landing at Plymouth, there were only three cows in New England.

In pre-historic times horses had developed in North America, but "had become extinct about the time the Indians first reached this continent" from Asia via the Bering Strait many centuries before Christ. American Indians never saw a horse until the Spaniards brought them over in the 1500s. These later became the mustangs of the western plains.

The ships from England and Holland were small and space was in great demand for other cargoes than livestock. However, for a hundred years or more the number of cattle grew along with the human population, but probably not as fast, due to the rising stream of immigrants from the old country. As to horses, there were very few in northern New England until after 1800.

For many years, while cattle and horses were bred, and calves and colts were growing up, the first settlers in the wilderness "grants" had to depend almost entirely on human muscle. Actually the pioneers were pack animals, with little but strong backs and stout hearts.

Consider the loads carried by these human pack animals. A settler in Poultney, Vermont, walked thirty miles to Manchester with one hundred pounds of iron on his back, and returned the next day with one hundred pounds of salt. He walked sixty miles for some groceries.

Colonel Crafts walked from Sturbridge, Massachusetts, to what is now Craftsbury, Vermont, a distance of one hundred and twenty miles. He drew his wife on a hand sled, "there being no road."

The first settlers in Newfane, Vermont, "without roads, horses or oxen, were under the necessity of conveying, by their own strength," all their provisions from Hinsdale, New Hampshire, a distance of thirty miles through a pathless wilderness. A little later two pioneers in Pomfret, Vermont, after harvesting their crop, walked home to Rehoboth, Rhode Island, a distance of about one hundred and eighty miles, in eleven days, and returned on foot the next spring. William Wilson came to the same town from Connecticut in 1771. A few weeks later his wife and three children "followed him the whole distance on foot." A Mr. Reed, of Troy, Vermont, on snowshoes, carried a plow on his back for twenty miles. Without much doubt similar feats of strength took place in every pioneer settlement.

There was a saying among the pioneers that a man who could not carry a hundred pounds on his back for ten miles was "not fit to begin a new settlement." Ira Allen and four others, running out of provisions in the wilderness, walked seventy miles to Pittsford in four days with no other food than one meal and three partridges. Deacon Burnap, of Lebanon, Connecticut, having "made his pitch" near Norwich, Vermont, walked home, assembled his wife and six children, "burdening each according to their several capacities," with the heaviest burden on his own shoulder. The whole family then "footed the entire distance back to Norwich," a distance of one hundred and forty miles as the crow flies, and many more by the twisting trails. Deacon Aiken and his hired man walked sixty-five miles "through dense forests and small settlements" from his home in Londonderry, New Hampshire, to Kent, Vermont (now Londonderry). During the summer he took sick, probably from malaria. Learning of his plight, his wife, carrying a nursing infant, rode horseback to her husband's side, nursed him back to health and then returned home as she had come.

Another settler in the same Vermont town, a butcher by trade, walked to his home in Boston when winter approached, returning on foot the next spring, and repeated this trip for twenty-two consecutive years. The distance was one hundred and twenty-five miles which he walked in two and one-half days. This equals fifty miles a day and seems almost incredible. However, in a much later history I learned that in 1917 James H. Hocking walked the ninety-seven miles from New York City to Philadelphia in nineteen hours and sixteen minutes, and that another man has walked thirty-two miles in four and one-half hours.

We can be sure that as the human tide moved slowly from the seacoast towns, men and women would not have carried heavy loads on their backs for many miles through the forests if other means had been available. Aside from their own muscle power, the only other sources of energy available to pioneers were the magnetic North Pole which gave direction to a compass; the chemical energy of gunpowder; the thermal energy of burning wood in the fireplace; the energy of gravity which made it easier to move men and cargoes down stream, and harder up stream or up hill; the energy of wind on the sails of ships, and the energy of the sun, of course, which causes the sap to rise and all living things to grow. I have read of only two windmills in early New England. Without energy, nothing is accomplished, even thinking.

For many centuries, animals carried burdens on their backs instead of hauling them. It was not until about 1100 A.D. that some genius invented a collar that enabled a horse to pull a heavy load for a task that took a long time, such as plowing a field. With this collar, horses pulled with their shoulders and not by a rope around their necks.

The wheel is said to be man's greatest invention. But as long as burdens were carried on human or animal backs, the wheel was a minor advance. It was the ox yoke and horse collar that made the wheel important. And I might add that these inventions marked the beginning of the end of human slavery. For pulling heavy loads, a horse or ox was equal to ten slaves. As has been said, the "greater tractability of the horse enlarged the frontiers of the world."*

* *The Picture History of Inventions* by Umberto Eco & G. B. Zorzoli, 1961.

[10]

As Others Saw Them

One of the few, and probably the best on-the-spot record of pioneer life in western New England in the late 1700s is that of the Rev. Nathan Perkins. He was the pastor of the Third Church of West Hartford, Connecticut (Congregational) and held that pastorate for sixty-six years. In 1789 he made a trip on horseback through western New England. He traveled alone. He left his home on April 17, went as far north as Burlington, Vermont, and returned home on June 11. Reverend Perkins was a child of the "Great Awakening" which was started in large part by the famous Jonathan Edwards. He was a founder of the Connecticut Missionary Society. This was his main reason for making the arduous trip.

I quote briefly from his diary, in his own spelling and old-fashioned use of words. The full text, entitled *A Narrative of a Tour through the State of Vermont*, has been published by the Charles E. Tuttle Co., of Rutland,

Vermont. If you read it you will be both saddened and amused.

As a strict Calvinist and the heir to a fortune, Parson Perkins had lived well. He liked hardly anything that he saw, heard, drank or ate on his trip. He was shocked by the uncouth manners, filthy homes and "infidelity" of the settlers. By infidelity he no doubt meant unfaithfulness to the precepts of the established church. Many of his judgments were harsh by today's standards. Yet he strove to be fair. He complimented the pioneers when he could, and toward the end of his trip began to question the virtues of the easy life of his own family and parishioners.

He visited about forty settlements in Massachusetts and Vermont, spending a day in each, and preaching whenever invited. He went through forty other townships that were uninhabited. "I have made more than a hundred miles and seen no meeting house [north of Bennington]." He preached in log huts, barns, or out of doors, wherever an audience would gather.

Pownal had a "miserable set of inhabitants—Rhode Island haters of religion," Bennington's "people, proud, scornful, conceited." At Sunderland "a raving arminian Methodist preached in ye evening. Here lived formerly ye awful Deist Ethan Allyn one of ye wickedest men ye ever walked this guilty Globe. . . . I looked at the grave with pious horror." (Allen had died the previous February.) At Middletown he found "wretched fare, wretched bed, eat up with fleas, no hay, my horse starving." At Brandon the "meanest of all lodging, dirty, fleas without number."

At New Haven, Vermont, he "preached at a log house—nothing but brook water to drink . . . slept in an open log house where it rained on me in ye night and no keeping [hay and oats] for my horse." At Williston he met Governor Chittenden. "A low, poor house—a low, vulgar man, clownish but made me welcome . . . a shrewd cunning man . . . understands extremely well ye mysteries of Vermont." Chittenden was Vermont's first Governor.

"Moose plenty on ye mountains . . . and wolves plenty . . . no beef, no butter. I pine for home, for my own table. . . . Far absent, among strangers, all alone, log huts, people nasty, low-lived, indelicate, and miserable cooks.

"Mud up to my horse's belly. Night came in, I could travel no farther. I found a little log hut and put up there, could get no supper, my horse no feed, slept on a chaff bed without covering, a man, his wife and three children all in ye same nasty stinking room.

"People pay little regard to ye Sabbath, hunt and fish on that day.

"People troubled with ye fever and ague.

"Many families have lived for weeks on what ye people call leeks, a sort of wild onion, very offensive to me. No candles, pine splinters used instead.

"In 1789 a year of calamity and famine . . . one fourth part of ye people will have neither bread nor meat for three weeks . . . several women had eight or ten children crying for bread and ye poor women had wept till they looked like Ghosts. O how happy am I at home, a paradise compared to Vermont. I grieve to hear what thousands and thousands have endured—women and children in coming to this state of Vermont."

His horse didn't like Vermont any better than he did, for at Essex "my horse got away and steered for Hartford, he had undergone hardships enough, he thought."

Despite the harshness of some of his judgments, the Reverend Perkins tried to be just. In fact he had words of admiration. For example, "Preached on ye Sabbath. A large audience deeply attentive . . . some very clever, serious and sensible. In a few years be a good Country, pleasant and well to live on."

"When I go from hut to hut, ye people nothing to eat, to drink, to wear, yet ye women serene, contented, loving their husbands, wanting never to return, nor any dressy clothes. . . .

"Woods make people love one another and be kind and obliging and good natured. They set much more store by one another than in ye old settlements.

"O how vile, how ungrateful to providence are our women [in his home town of Hartford]. Tell lies about one another, envy one another, dress and enjoy fine roads, carriages and husbands to wait on them and yet uneasy, unaffectionate . . . could my Lady [his wife] only see and endure what I have, how contented, how thankful would she be . . . she would feel a rapture of gratitude to heaven for our happy lot."

This diary makes more credible the harsh difficulties that confronted Seth Hubbell. He and Reverend Perkins must have followed the same wilderness trail much of the way. In April and May the minister's horse twice had to go through "mud up to his belly" and "swam over deep streams." This helps to explain why Hubbell started his trip in wintertime when the ground was frozen.

Many times in the spring and growing season of the year, the clergyman's horse found little or no grass; no hay and of course no oats. "My horse was deeply grieved," wrote the clergyman, and "my ox failed," wrote the old soldier.

[11]

Why They Came

"Westward the course of empire took its way." This has been true of the great migrations of people in Europe, Asia, and in North America itself. But following the surrender by France in 1763 of all claims to territory east of the Mississippi, the magnetic needle of migration swerved northward and inland. Nearly all the settlers in Maine, New Hampshire and Vermont left homes in Massachusetts, Rhode Island and Connecticut. In fact, Vermont was first officially named "New Connecticut."

Why did the tide of migration turn to the north? It could not have been due to population pressure. In 1791, Connecticut, for example, had only 237,000 inhabitants, whereas in 1960 it had 2,535,000, or over ten times as many. But the white men pushed north in an ever-increasing flood. Some people think that the settlers were fools to go to hilly, rock-strewn country rather than to the "rich, flat and rock-free meadow lands" west of the Alleghenies. These critics do not know the economics of transportation. The narrow wagon trails westward were almost impassable in winter and spring mud. And even in dry weather, transportation costs by ox-team were prohibitive. It was not until 1806 that Congress authorized the construction of the "Cumberland Road" across the Alleghenies, and it was 1833 before it got as far as Columbus, Ohio.

As for railroads, they did not begin serious construction until 1828. It was 1853 before the Baltimore & Ohio Railroad Company linked Baltimore with Wheeling, West Virginia. The westward course of empire from New England did not really get under way until the construction of the Erie Canal in 1825. This linked New York City to Buffalo and the West via the Hudson River and the Great Lakes. Water transportation of heavy cargoes reduced the cost from thirty-two dollars a ton per hundred miles, to one dollar or less. It was not until 1855 that New York City and Chicago were linked by rail.

While this explains the logic of northward migration in the late 1700s and early 1800s, it does not tell why the settlers moved at all. There was no one reason, but probably a dozen. Why did Seth Hubbell and other pioneers go to northern Vermont? There were several reasons that we know of, any one of which might have influenced the settlers. Although there was plenty of land left in lower New England, nevertheless as it became settled it began to have greater money value. Hence it was logical for the younger generation to think of the practically free land in northern New England as

74

a better place to start their lives. Also there was a continuing heavy demand for lumber of all sorts to export to England and Europe for the "King's Navy," and after the Revolutionary War ended, for merchantmen, fishing and whaling boats operating out of the New England seaports, and the winter heating of homes in New England. The nearby forests were naturally the first to become thinned out, with the result that men moved north to the still primeval forests of upper New England. For some years the small town of Burlington, Vermont, on Lake Champlain, was the largest lumber exporting town in the United States, the lumber moving by water northward to the St. Lawrence River and thence to the Atlantic Ocean and the world.

Fur trapping was a major occupation in New England for a long time. The skins of the deer, fox, bear, mink, sable, marten, fisher, raccoon and beaver were in great demand. As late as the Civil War, a beaver hat was a gentleman's prized possession, handed down from father to son. As the forests were cleared in lower New England, the wild animals moved northward and the white men followed. As long as there was plenty of wild game, including fish, the pioneers could live until forests were cleared and crops were grown. Potash was a very valuable article of commerce. Again, as the forests of lower New England, from which potash was made, were cut down, the potash trade moved to the north, and men and women followed.

The laws of inheritance probably influenced some of the migration to Maine, Vermont and New Hampshire. The old English system of primogeniture and entail of land to the oldest son never got firmly rooted in New England. Nevertheless, the laws of Massachusetts and Connecticut provided that when a man died intestate, his oldest son inherited a double portion of the land, subject of course to the widow's dower. This meant that the oldest son got twice as much land, in value, as each of his younger brothers. If, for example, there were two sons, the elder got two-thirds of the land and the younger one-third. Daughters inherited no land if there were sons. They were limited to the personal property. These laws of inheritance did not promote brotherly love. They were bound to make the younger sons and daughters, and the wives of the sons, unhappy with their lot.

The Vermont legislature, on the other hand, as early as 1779, provided that, subject to the widow's dower, the sons and daughters should have "equal portions" in value of the real and personal estate. The sons were to have their portions in land, so far as the property would allow, and the daughters their equal portions in the personal property. If there were no sons, daughters inherited the land as "coparceners" (joint owners).

Without getting into the merits of one religious creed as against another, it is plain that many young people in the late 1700s were breaking away from the more severe precepts of Calvinism, as set forth by the great divine, the Rev. Jonathan Edwards, who was pastor of the leading church in Northampton, Massachusetts, for many years. Infant damnation, except for divine grace alone, seemed too extreme to many, and particularly to the younger members of a community. Evidently a substantial rift developed between the elder and more church-going folk in Connecticut and the younger generation that was pioneering in Vermont.

The slow trickle of the first settlers northward was turned into a flood by important political events. The most important was the signing of the peace treaty with Great Britain on September 3, 1783. This not only ended British claims on American territory, but quieted the fears of further raids and massacres by the Indians as allies of Great Britain. It likewise terminated all authority, whether actual or claimed, by the royal governors of New Hampshire over the New Hampshire Grants, as Vermont was then called, and the title to its land.

But New York continued to claim title to all of Vermont! Her royal governors had issued "grants" to Vermont land, as New Hampshire had done. New York continued to assert her claims after the Treaty of Peace with Great Britain and opposed Vermont's desire to be admitted to the Union. Finally, on October 28, 1790, Vermont paid New York thirty thousand dollars to settle her claims to Vermont land. Four months later Vermont was admitted to the Union as the fourteenth state.

With these questions settled, the pioneers considered their land titles to be safe, and poured into Vermont, almost doubling its population in ten years.

In Massachusetts a high land tax worked especial hardship on farmers in comparison with taxes paid chiefly by merchants and townspeople. This led to Shay's Rebellion in 1786–87. A former captain in the

Revolutionary Army, Daniel Shay led one thousand angry men to seize the Worcester and Springfield courthouses to prevent the courts from enforcing contracts or state laws for debt. The Governor mustered an army of four thousand men which routed the rebels after a few were killed. Daniel Shay fled to Vermont, and many followed. In New Hampshire a mob of farmers surrounded the legislature and demanded the repeal of taxes and the issuance of paper money.

These rebellions disturbed the general public, and there was so much sympathy for the rebels that many public officials who had helped put down a rebellion were defeated at the polls when they ran for re-election. General Washington wrote that "the prejudices, jealousies and turbulence of the people at times almost stagger my confidence in our political establishments."

Another reason Vermont was attractive to settlers from other New England states was its conservative monetary policy as viewed against the catastrophic inflation that swept the thirteen states during and after the Revolution. Vermont was officially a separate nation from the time of its own Declaration of Independence on January 17, 1777, until she joined the Union in 1791. She had no part or responsibility, therefore, in the flood of paper money issued by the Continental Congress, or by any of the thirteen states.

"Not worth a continental" was the reproach attached to the so-called dollars of paper money. In Virginia, by 1781, this currency fell to one thousand for one dollar in hard money. Foreigners bought five thousand dollars worth of Continental scrip for a single dollar of gold.

How did this affect the ordinary citizen? Uriel Cross came to Vermont from Connecticut with four hundred and eighty-seven dollars in silver which he had saved during three years of hard work. Desiring to join the Green Mountain Boys under Col. Remember Baker, he was advised to exchange his hard (and heavy) money for Continental currency. This he did. When his army service ended a couple of years later, he had to exchange seventy-two dollars of paper currency for one dollar in silver coin. His original four hundred and eighty-seven dollars in silver had therefore shrunk to about seven dollars. As he bemoaned, "In this way I did worse than to sit down and done nothing."

Old Tom Chittenden, Vermont's first governor, who served for seventeen years and had only one eye, could not see how a government could make its people affluent by printing dollar signs on pieces of paper and making them legal tender! He was a conservative in money matters. Vermont coined its own hard money and did not go head-over-heels in debt. Its legislature decreed that counterfeiters should "suffer death"; nothing less. This was later softened to forfeiture of the counterfeiter's entire estate, cutting off his right ear, branding him with a hot iron with the letter "C" and imprisoning him for life. This was strong medicine, but it created confidence in the new Republic and undoubtedly influenced migration to the state.

$\lceil 12 \rceil$

Log Cabins

There is no more solid fixture in American folklore than the log cabin. To have been born in one has been a prime political asset to office seekers from constable to president.

Six Americans who were born in log cabins became presidents of the United States. Abraham Lincoln is, of course, the best known. Before him was Andrew Jackson, who was born in 1767, the only one of the six who had been a British subject. He was elected President in 1828. He was followed by Presidents Polk, Pierce, Buchanan, Lincoln and Garfield, who became President in 1881.

Before Lincoln was elected in 1860 there was William Henry Harrison. He was not born in a log cabin but was living in a house that was half log cabin when he was elected. His campaign was the most rollicking and hilarious in American history. Parades and floats carrying small log cabins with latch string out and a cider barrel

Building their wilderness home.

by the door helped give Harrison two hundred and thirty-four electoral votes to sixty for Van Buren.

The magic of the log cabin has worked its spell to our own time. In the 1930s a friend of mine, born in a log cabin in Indiana, served with me in Congress. It was therefore painful to me to learn that the log cabin is not an American invention. There was none in what is now New England for twenty years or more after Plymouth Rock. This, despite the Mayflower Pilgrims being at the edge of the greatest forest in the New World. The first settlers at Plymouth, Jamestown, Salem, etc., and their ancestors in the old country, had probably never seen log cabins and consequently never thought of building them.

Astonishing as this may seem today, there were reasons for this. England and the low countries of Europe had been short of timber for a long time. Demand exceeded supply. British forests were being cut down to make charcoal, without which iron, lead and glass could not be made. Holland, which built and armed more ships than all the rest of Europe, was "not possessed of a foot of timber." She had to depend on imported lumber. Trevelyan in his *English Social History* reports that around 1675, "cow dung, that ought to have enriched the fields, was gathered and dried for fuel" in England.

As an island kingdom, England had to have scores of wooden ships. In England's long struggle with France and Spain for the mastery of the Atlantic and of North America, timber for ships had priority over other claims. In her most fateful sea battle in history, the defeat of the Spanish Armada in 1588, England had a fleet of one hundred and ninety-seven wooden ships. Britain's need for ships is highlighted in our own history by the commandeering of New England's tallest and best pine trees to be used for masts and timber for the King's Navy and merchant ships. There were of course some forests still left in England in 1620 when the Mayflower dropped anchor at Plymouth. But forests were "off limits" to common folk. The feudal lords needed them for hunting deer. The common people had to live in huts, or small cottages made of sod, turf, stone and the like.

The red men knew nothing of log cabins because they were still living in the "stone age." They had no iron and hence no metal axes or saws. Most Indian shelters in New England were wigwams, made by thrusting saplings into the ground in a circle, pulling their tops together in the form of a dome and tying them with twisted wild grass or the branches of saplings. They were covered with animal hides or bark from elm, birch, or other trees, and then plastered with mud or clay to keep out the rain and snow. White settlers occasionally made temporary shelters similar to wigwams.

Sometimes the first months in the wilderness were spent by settlers in dugouts in the sides of hills or in caves. The famous Ann Story of Vermont had, in addition to her house, a cave hideaway on the bank of the Otter Creek.

The historians seem to agree that the idea of log cabins came over with the Swedes who first settled in Delaware around 1638, some eighteen years after Plymouth Rock. The Scandinavian countries had plenty of forests and their people were accustomed to cabins and houses made of logs. So they built them on this side of the Atlantic, and the idea spread like wildfire to New England and elsewhere. A log cabin, however crude, was a sturdy shelter. A good axe-man alone in the forest could make a log cabin without help except for hauling the logs to the selected site and lifting them into place. At the corners of the building, the logs were notched together like clasped fingers and held in place by their weight.* The only tools absolutely essential were an axe, a whetsone and an auger. The auger bored holes into which wooden tree nails called "trunnels" were driven. Iron nails were not to be had.

The famous Eleazer Wheelock started the college that became Dartmouth in the New Hampshire wilderness in 1770 by building a "hut" of logs for his family. It was eighteen feet square "without stone, brick, glass or nails." His nearest neighbor was over two miles away. "I see nothing but lofty pines about me," he said.

With the large number of children in those "good old days," the cabins were generally crowded. And sometimes there were other families and friends. A classic case of crowding is that of Jonathan Perham and Ephraim Holden, of Rindge, New Hampshire. In the dead of winter in 1780 they and their families took possession of an abandoned log hut in Athens, Vermont. Shortly after, they were joined by a third family, that of Seth Oakes from Winchendon, Massachusetts. Mrs. Oakes gave birth to a daughter, the first born in the township.

* See illustrations in *Museum of Early Tools* by Eric Sloane, pp. 24–25, 1964.

The thirty or forty trees needed to build a small cabin paid three dividends. One was the cabin itself. Another was the clearing made in the forest where the trees had been cut down. The land had to be cleared anyway for the growing of crops. Third, the pioneers needed wood to cook their food and to keep warm. The pioneer, unlike his ancestors, had all the wood he could burn. Nothing gave him greater happiness than a roaring fire. In this respect, at least, he need skimp no more.

[13]

How Towns Grew

It is worthwhile to note the general sequence of events
by which the first settlers and those who followed
turned a wilderness into a community. The time taken
by this sequence was generally about a quarter of a century, but in some cases, ten years longer. This is the
period covered by this book.

Shelter, of course, came first for man and beast. The
priority of necessity determined what was then done by
one family, or with others as they joined forces for the
larger tasks. This sequence and the time consumed can
be illustrated by a small town in southern Vermont:
Jamaica, in Windham County:

> The first clearing, 1775
> Five years later, eleven families
> First town meeting, 1781
> First saw mill, 1783
> First grist mill (probably in the same
> building) 1783

A one-room schoolhouse.

First road built through the town, wider than
a trail 1784
First log schoolhouse, 1791
First tavern, 1793
First church group of eight members, having
a pastor, 1794
First church building, 1808
First resident physician, 1815
First post office, 1819

About the time of the first mill, someone probably
started the first blacksmith shop; another a "potash
works," and a third, a general store. Those were the
"hard scrabble" years. The first school or organized
teaching of children did not come until sixteen years
after the first settlement. The first church building had
to wait thirty-three years. The town was without a
resident physician for its first forty years, and without
a post office for forty-four years. The length of time
taken for this development in the different New England
towns depended largely on access to markets and the
means and cost of transportation. It was one thing to
move heavy objects, such as a grindstone, by ox cart or
winter sled, and another to move them by boat. The
seaport towns grew first and fastest because they were
on salt water. And the hardships of pioneer life were
often separated by only a few miles from the comforts
of colonial living.

The earliest pioneers had no money. The British
government forbade them to have gold or silver coins,
even in British money. Colonial paper money was not

authorized in Massachusetts before 1690, and when it was issued, it fluctuated widely in value. Even after the Revolution there was not much money around. When Seth Hubbell and his family were desperately in need of food, he caught and skinned a sable and then walked fifty miles before he found someone who would trade wheat for it. "Trading posts" were the only places having some slight resemblance to the general store which developed later. But trading posts were few and generally many miles away. And even when settlements were established and general stores became more common, buying and selling was done mostly on a barter basis.

[14]

Light and Heat

"The flint missed fire." The gun did not shoot. The owner of the gun died—perhaps from the claws of a bear, or the return fire of an Indian, as did the famous Remember Baker, Ethan Allen's close relative. The flintlock musket of the pioneers depended upon a spark ignited by the friction of steel on flint as the trigger was pulled. The spark had to reach the priming powder in the flash pan before it expired a second later. Hence the name "firearm" and the expression "hold your fire."

But the chief need of a pioneer family was heat and light, and a method similar to that of the musket was used. Holding a flint in the left hand and striking it sharply downward with a piece of iron or steel, one could hope that a spark would fall into the tinder box and ignite. The tinder had to be a very dry, inflammable substance such as partially charred linen cloth. Under the best of circumstances striking a fire was a painstaking job. Vermont's famous judge, Wendell Phillips Stafford, in his address on Ann Story, spoke of "the settler crouching by his hearth where the last faint ember has expired, trying with infinite pains to bring the birth of fire from the cold marriage of flint and steel." One historian of colonial days wrote that she had struck flint with steel hundreds of times without success. Charles Dickens, who visited the United States in 1857, said that with luck he could strike fire in a half hour or so. Hence the expression "strike a light."

Suppose the room was below zero and snow driven through the roof and walls of the log cabin had made everything damp. Or that the flint was lost. Or that there was no dry wood.

Providing plenty of dry wood was one of the most demanding jobs of the settlement. Windfall trees, or standing but dead trees, were selected for cutting when available as they were at least partly free from sap. They were then "snaked" from the woods by oxen. They were cut into fireplace length, split when necessary and kept under cover if possible. A shed or roof over the wood was almost as important as the wood itself. If there were no shed, the firewood could be piled in a long row and covered with bark to keep off the snow and rain as much as possible. To heat a cabin all winter and to cook and wash dishes and clothes all year required fifteen to twenty cords of wood. If cut and piled in a single row, in cord-wood width, length and height, the wood pile would be one hundred and twenty to one hundred and sixty feet long.

Try starting a fire without a match sometime. Hold a piece of steel against a revolving grindstone, or abrasive wheel. You will get a continuous stream of sparks, not just two or three, to land on your dry tinder or tissue paper. If they "catch" in less than a dozen tries you will do well. You will understand pioneer life better if you try to make a fire as they did. It has been said that "fire is the most important agent of civilization."

Friction matches are one of man's greatest inventions. But there were none before 1827. In firearms the percussion cap was not invented until 1807. It superseded the flintlock in time, but "Old Betsey" continued to be used up to the Civil War.

Return now to a pioneer family in their log cabin in New England. It was very important when they banked the fire for the night to cover some of the live embers with ashes. Cut off from much of the oxygen, the embers could be expected to keep "alive" until morning when they could be uncovered and blown into a blazing fire. If the embers died during the night, or the family went away for several days, it was necessary to again resort to flint and steel, or send someone to the nearest neighbor to borrow some live coals and bring them back in a fire "scoop." If the nearest neighbor was miles away, and the snow lay three feet deep, the pioneer family had a real problem, especially if it was zero weather. Sometimes pioneers froze to death.

Boy Scouts know there is another way to start a fire which was used by the Indians. That is to use the friction of a rapidly revolving dry stick of wood, one end resting in a hole in another piece of wood. The point of contact of the two pieces can get hot enough to start a flame. I have found no mention of any pioneer using this method, but do not doubt that it was used when flint and steel were missing. Apart from sunlight, firelight was the only light the pioneers had when they first settled in the wilderness. They went to bed at dark and got up at dawn. Later on light was produced in the cabins by burning torches made of pitch pine, or the pith of dried rushes soaked in grease. A grease-soaked rush or rag was used in a "betty lamp," a small container usually made of iron, with a vertical handle. Candles came next, made by tying wicks of hemp, tow or silk down from milkweed to a wand and dipping them in hot wax until the desired thickness was reached. Animal fats were used, but they were unpleasant to smell and gave a poor light. Wax from a beehive or from bayberries made the best candles.

[15]

Honey Bees

Seventy per cent of the American people are now living on about one per cent of the land. This one per cent is used chiefly to hold up buildings and not for the purposes for which forest and meadow were mainly used by our forefathers. Today this seventy per cent can probably see no point whatever in the question one man asked another in 1782. "Have you seen any bees yet?"* That was, and still is, about as important a question as any that could be asked today by anyone, anywhere. Bees are basic. By bees I mean honey bees.

When the white men came to New England in 1620 there were no honey bees, just as there were no cows, sheep, oxen, or horses. Forest trees can live for centuries without honey bees. But there are very few meadow and orchard crops, such as clover and apples, that can reproduce themselves on a large scale without honey bees. It is said that without bees "there would not be enough food for the largest percentage of the people in the world

* *Letters from an American Farmer* by J. Hector St. John de Crevecoeur, 1782.

94

today." This means that more than half the world's people would feel the pinch of extreme hunger, and if invention did not somehow come to the rescue, hordes of them would die. One hundred thousand species of flowering plants would disappear from the earth.

Mankind's whole food structure in the vegetable kingdom is based on pollination resulting in the union of the male and female elements in the production of seeds. Only a relatively few plants are self-pollinating. Most depend on cross-pollination by the wind, birds, or burrs attaching themselves to the family dog or other animals. Chiefly, however, cross-pollination is done by insects which of course include wasps, hornets and yellow jackets. Some eighty per cent of the insects visiting an orchard or meadow today are honey bees. They are the important insects, first, because they are such busy workers and second, because their hives can be moved bodily into the orchards and meadows when they are in blossom. An acre of apple trees, for example, has a million blossoms inviting the honey bees to suck their nectar. In doing so, pollen rubs off on the bees and is carried to other blossoms. "Nectar is the fee paid by the plant for the fertilizing service of the bees."

Only eighteen years after Plymouth Rock honey bees began to be imported from the Old World to New England. The Indians had never seen them and called them "white men's flies." They multiplied very fast and apparently kept a little ahead of the pioneers as they moved into the great forest. One reason the Indians never be-

* *The World of Bees* by Murray Hoyt, 1965.

came an agricultural people, in addition to their lack of iron tools, is that they never had the benefit of honey bees. In New England the bees became a principal source of sweets and also wax from which candles were made. It must have been a great comfort to the settler and his hard-working wife to have ten or twenty thousand or more "farm hands" working for them without charge! To keep the bees, or new swarms of them, from hiving in hollow trees where they were hard to get at, they were often provided with a home called a "skep," or hive made of tightly braided straw in the shape of an upside-down basket. When cold weather came, they were put under cover.

When I was a boy, we put the hives in the attic over the woodshed. There they had some protection from the bitter cold. They were kept dry, with plenty to eat. All winter long I liked to go up near the hives and listen to the never ending musical hum of the busy little people. And what a delight it must have been to the pioneer's wife way back in the old days, when a lilac slip which she had carried from her former home "down country," brought forth its first blossom at the cabin door, and on it a busy honey bee! It was a sign of better times to come. The pioneers were kind to honey bees. They could not have known what scientific men know today— that the bees that produce one pound of honey for you to enjoy have flown a distance of once or twice around the world. New England folklore tells us that in an Indian raid against a white man's village, they knocked over a beehive. This made the bees very angry and the Indians very scarce.

[16]

No Salt

The old-time histories and gazetteers record at great length the presence of scores of minerals, including specks of gold, but not one mentions salt deposits in New England. Stranger still, I find no expression of wonder that salt was never found. For salt is indispensable to the life and livelihood of man and beast. Therefore, to the chapter "No Grass" we add "No Salt." By that we mean rock salt—sodium chloride such as is found today on every kitchen table in America and in thousands of barns and pasture lots.

You may say, "But surely there were salt licks where pools of brackish water had evaporated on the surface of the ground and left a sediment that could be licked up by wild and domestic animals." The only "salt lick" I have found mentioned was at Bridport, Vermont. But it was not sodium chloride. It was sulphate of magnesia, which is a purgative known as Epsom Salts. Indispensable as salt is today, it was equally so when the white men came. It must be remembered that before Plymouth

Rock (1620), fishermen on the seacoast of what is now New England had a large foreign trade with Europe and the West Indies. That trade consisted chiefly of salt water fish, cod, halibut and salmon, and furs of all kinds, which required huge quantities of salt to keep the fish edible and to cure the hides, pelts and skins of beavers, deer, moose, bears, martens, sables, foxes, etc. Without salt there would have been no foreign trade in fish and furs and the settlement of New England would have been postponed for many years.

Fortunately, the same ships that carried fish and furs to markets overseas returned loaded with salt. This solved the problem for New England's seacoast towns. It was, however, another matter for the pioneers who chose the forest and not the sea. They had to have a brine barrel also for salt pork and pickles, salt for butter and hams. They also had to cure the hides of animals to make leather for boots, "britches," harness, snowshoes and dozens of other articles. The settlers' cattle were fond of salt and if they could lick a cake of salt at home they seldom wandered far. In the absence of salt they were apt to wander miles from home, and the time spent in the search for them was a great aggravation to the pioneers.

The transportation of imported salt from the seacoast towns to the homes on the hills was a costly operation. Salt is heavy; it must be kept dry and needs tight containers. Salt was an expensive necessity; how expensive we cannot tell for the value of money has changed many times since pioneer days. However, I find that Jonathan Dike, of Chittenden, Vermont, brought a bushel of salt from Bennington, a distance of about sixty miles, and was offered a bushel of corn for each pint of salt. On a volume basis this put the value of salt at about sixty-four times that of corn. Salt was at all times scarce and at no time available to the pioneers except at prices which were almost prohibitive. In the 1790s huge deposits of salt, some of which were hundreds of feet deep, were found in the Onondaga district, near Syracuse, New York. But even then, in the absence of water transportation, until the Erie Canal was opened in 1825, salt was a long, hard and heavy haul by ox-cart over rough roads.

It might be asked why the early settlers did not get salt from the Atlantic Ocean which was right at their door. The settlers did try to do so many times, but without success. The ocean is about three per cent salt, which means that it took about three hundred and fifty gallons of sea water to produce a bushel of salt. The salt can be separated only by evaporation by the heat of the sun, which costs nothing, or by burning fuel, which is expensive. Huge pans or vats must be used with protection from rainfall. All such efforts ended in financial failure. However, beginning about 1700, salt was, and still is, produced by solar evaporation on the Turks and Caicos Islands in the British West Indies. But there the average temperature is about eighty degrees, which is ten or fifteen degrees hotter than New England. Also, the average yearly rainfall is almost a foot less than on the New England coast. Turks Island ocean salt was, in fact, one source of supply to New England. But most of the salt was imported from the Old World, coming from deposits in England and the continent.

$\begin{bmatrix} 1\,7 \end{bmatrix}$

Potash

The first settlers in the "up-country" towns of New England had a "potash works" that served them well for a couple of generations and then, when it seemed to be a permanent source of income, it vanished. These "works" were the pioneers' first manufacturing industry and the first source of "hard money" except for the fur trade and the tall pine trees fit for ship masts that grew close enough to navigable rivers to be floated down to the sea.

As the forest trees were cut down, most of those not used for log cabins and fuel were burned to ashes. This helped to get rid of the tree trunks and branches so that crops could be planted. But equally important, the ashes were valuable in themselves. They were collected and slowly leached with water, which produced a dark liquid called lye, or potassium carbonate, a strong alkali. The lye was then poured into huge iron pots at the "works" and the water in the lye was boiled out, leaving a grey, dry, friable anhydrous powder or crystals called potash,

Leaching the ashes into lye.

or pearl ash. The word *potash* came from the huge iron pots in which the lye was boiled dry. As a young man in Connecticut, Ethan Allen was a pot maker, and one of the absolutely essential articles brought by every settler to his new home in the wilderness was an iron pot. It took about four hundred and fifty bushels of ashes to make one ton of potash. There were huge quantities of ashes as the trees were cut down and burned. For days on end in spring and summer "the atmosphere was filled and the sun obscured by smoke."

In nearly every town with a dozen families or more, there was a "potash works." This made it possible for a number of pioneers to co-operate in leaching the lye from its ashes and boiling the water out of the lye to produce the potash. The huge, heavy iron pots were often beyond the financial means of a single family, being much bigger than the household iron pot in which much of the cooking was done. When I was a boy, the "works" were long since gone, but many a farm home, as late as 1910, had a barrel of ashes under the eaves that caught rain water to leach their own lye, just as their great-grandfathers and mothers had done. They boiled the lye with hog fats and kitchen greases and produced a thick liquid soft soap. By further boiling, it became hard soap which was cut into cakes like today's "store" soap. After washing one's hands with this home-made soap, it was advisable to rinse well or "the alkali will tell you why."

From the first settlements until 1825 or so, potash was in great demand in the manufacture of woolen cloth, linen, glass, etc., both here and abroad. It became a prime source of income. As soon as enough people had settled in a township to have a general store, potash was accepted by the storekeeper and credited against the purchase price of pins, needles, tobacco, West India rum, tea and other commodities. Many of the early stores had small buildings in the rear where potash was stored until enough was on hand to be drayed by ox-team or carried by boat to Boston, Albany or Montreal. In some cases the storekeeper "took in trade" the wood ashes and made the potash himself.

Even if the nearest store was ten or twenty miles distant, potash had the great advantage of being so light in weight, in proportion to its value, that a substantial money's worth could be carried to the store on a man's back, or by a hand sled in winter, to be exchanged for "boughten goods." Potash was in great demand abroad. Excepting fish, furs and ship timber, it was New England's first important export. English woolen mills needed it so badly that Parliament, as early as 1751, exempted it from import duties. This was distinctly the reverse of its policy regarding all other American manufactured products. British and French mills needed American potash because their own forests had been generally denuded by generations of wood cutting. Manuals on how to make potash were prepared abroad and scattered far and wide over New England.

In 1791 Vermont produced one thousand tons of potash. A single county produced three hundred tons or six hundred thousand pounds that year. Exports to England and France grew rapidly. In 1790 potash worth $840,000 was exported from America, chiefly from the New England states. This was equal to about $4,000,000 today. Potash enjoyed a seller's market for half a century. Writing in 1809, Vermont's famous historian, Samuel Williams, said that "the mountains will not fail to supply wood for this manufacture for centuries yet to come." Land values went up as the trees came down. New England was riding high. Then the roof fell in. In the early 1800s European scientists learned that sodium could be used in place of potash, and be produced from huge salt deposits in Alsace, Germany and Austria. That turned the tide and European potash, or rather its equivalent, was soon being imported into the United States.

[18]

Stray Beasts

One of the constant problems and irritations of the pioneers was the tendency of their domestic animals—oxen, cows, sheep, hens and hogs—to wander far afield. This also irritated the owner of the land they wandered onto, especially if it was a field or orchard where crops were growing. During the first hectic years there was more important work to do than to spend time building fences and stone walls. Many years went by before the pioneer's "pitch" was well fenced. And even when fences were "horse high, ox strong and hog tight," domestic animals still escaped. With animals, as with men, the "grass always looks greener on the other side of the fence." Later, when fences were built or stone walls laid, the old timers put "pokes" on cattle to make it hard for them to jump over or through a fence. A poke was any device fastened around the neck of an animal that would catch in a fence as the beast attempted to push through, or jump over it. Another stratagem was to not completely wean a spring calf until the end of autumn. As a result, the calf, kept in the barnyard, was always hungry and bawling for its mother. This was more than the mother could stand, and toward evening she would come home to her calf. The other cattle generally followed.

Stray beasts were so common that most towns built a "pound" and chose a pound keeper. A pound was an enclosed space with high walls around it in which strays were "impounded." If the owner were known or could be found, he was notified to get his beast and pay the cost of catching and feeding it.

To help identify the stray animals they were generally marked by various "crops" on the animal's horns or ears. This served the same purpose as the brands by which cattlemen in the West marked their animals. These markings helped to identify stolen animals, and made it more risky to steal them.

A description of the mark was frequently recorded with the town clerk. This helped the finder of a stray beast to notify the owner. Samples of these records, taken from the *History of Salem, N.H.*, (1907) are as follows:

> May ye 8th 1753. The marks of Cattel and other cretrs.
> Abiel Astens mark of his cattel and other cretrs is a halpny ye undr sid of ye laft ear and a halpny ye upr sid of ye right ear.
> March ye 15, 1754 the marks of Alexandr Gordens Cattel and other creachers is a crop of ye right ear & a half crop of ye upper sid of ye ner ear.

The marks of Jonathan Wheler junr Cattel & other crechers is a Swalows taill in ye off ear & too Slits in ye Eand of ye ner ear.

If there was no pound, the finder could keep the stray in his own barnyard and post a notice describing the animal with the town clerk. For example:

Eantrd hear by ordr of Captn Richard Kaley A Sartrn brindel ox somthing high horns coming in six yers old as he soposes branded on one horne with too aches (H H) and too kase (K's) above ye aches & a sort of a crop of ye near ear pounded July ye 28, 1746 by Captn Kaley.

The near ear was the left one. This comes from the fact that a yoke of oxen was driven by a man walking on the left side of the team. This was because most men are right handed and it is easier for them to use a stick or whip to guide a yoke of oxen from the left of the team, while telling them to "gee" (go right), "haw" (go left) or "whoa" (stop).

$\lceil 19 \rceil$

To Have and To Hold

Suppose there were a good, dry path around the earth at the Equator and that a man six feet tall walked the entire distance. Did his head and feet travel the same distance? This brain twister appears in a book on surveying published a century and a half ago. It was designed to warn young surveyors to be very careful.

In 1709 the British Parliament enacted the first "enclosure bill." It freed a small land area from "common use" and permitted private ownership "to have and to hold." These words or their equivalent are now in warranty deeds everywhere. This was the beginning of the end of serfs, cotters and peasants in Old England. But a century went by before private ownership of British soil became almost universal in the old country. On this side of the Atlantic, the emigrants from England demanded the right "to have and to hold" by all men, regardless of rank or title. They wanted the right to build fences and stone walls around land that was to be their very own and to tell trespassers to keep out. It is true that some

New England villages had the common use of small meadows or pastures which later became public parks or greens, even as Boston Common. But this was more a matter of convenience and protection. As is well known, the Plymouth Pilgrims gave up the common ownership of land as a bad job three years after landing.

The pioneers had a fierce hunger for private ownership of land. Certainly they would not have penetrated the dark forest wilderness and spent a lifetime of hard work converting the forests into meadows if they had no assurance that they and their wives and children would possess the land, "to have and to hold" against all comers. This hunger also had something to do with the signing of the Declaration of Independence. Who would sow where others could reap? The landowner had to know where his boundaries were, where he could build stone walls and fences to keep his own animals in and other animals out. In short, his land had to be surveyed and its boundaries marked—accurately.

Under the conditions of three or even two centuries ago this was an almost impossible task. It is hard enough today. "Good fences make good neighbors," as Robert Frost said, but if the "line" is in dispute, a perfect fence makes no one happy. The disputes were not all between individual landowners. They were also between towns, counties, states and even school districts. These public bodies were often parties to boundary disputes from their right to tax disputed land, or their burden of building bridges and highways or even whether a child should be taught in one school or another.

The chief instruments in making surveys were the

109

compass to measure direction and the "Gunter chain" to measure distance. The magnetic needle of the compass was often deflected by iron deposits scattered over New England and seldom pointed true north. The Gunter chain, invented in England about the time the Pilgrims landed in 1620, was a chain of one hundred wire links sixty-six feet, or four rods, long. Eighty chains made a mile ($66 \times 80 = 5,280$ feet) and ten square chains made an acre ($66 \times 66 \times 10 = 43,560$ square feet). The chain was pulled straight by two men at the ends but it always had a sag from its own weight which shortened it a trifle less than sixty-six feet. It was also longer or shorter depending on the temperature, much like the rails of a railroad. Such differences were slight, but repeated all day long or a hundred miles long, the total error was enough to quarrel over.

It was for such reasons that the old-time deeds often read "more or less." The grantor and grantee might intend to sell and buy a square mile of land, six hundred and forty acres, but the true acreage was not guaranteed. There were other obstacles. How do you carry a chain across or around a twenty acre beaver pond, or a huge boulder, or a steep cliff that is in the direction you wish to go? Worse, however, was the disappearance of surveyors' markers because of trees rotting, or streams changing course, or forest fires burning over hundreds of acres, or a "beech tree seven inches in diameter" which blew down in a hurricane twenty years ago. If the "confluence of Hinkley Brook and Saxtons River," the agreed marker many years ago, was moved somewhere else in a flood, what do you or your neighbor, do?

Here is the actual case of a survey made in 1741 based on a royal decree that was to fix the northern boundary of Massachusetts coinciding with New Hampshire's southern boundary. (A large part of what is now Vermont was then in New Hampshire.) According to an old history, a survey was run by the compass and "ten degrees were allowed for the westerly variation of the magnetic needle." This was too great an allowance with the result that New Hampshire lost 59,873 acres and what is now Vermont lost 133,897 acres. It took a half century of "jawing" and hard feeling to get the three states to agree to the present boundary line.

This may be the source of the story of an old Vermont farmer who lived on the land in dispute which his father and grandfather had occupied for eighty years before him. In time a surveying team with their compasses and Gunter chains ran back and forth across the old man's hills and meadows. After a week of this, the surveyors came to the old farmer and told him that a mistake had been made in the old survey, and they were awfully sorry to have to tell him that his farm was in Massachusetts. The old man said "nary a word" but kept on shaving fire lighting splinters from a stick of basswood. The young surveyors had expected him to explode.

They said, "It's too bad, grandpa, but it's bully of you to take this sad news so well."

He said, "Don't let it worry you, boys. Fact is, I never did like them Vermont winters none too well, and I'll be glad to live in Massachusetts."

111

[20]

Wild Animals

"It was wisely and kindly provided by the Creator to answer the immediate needs of the first settlers." This statement by the famous Timothy Dwight, who was president of Yale College in the late 1700s, is confirmed by Amos Story, the husband of Vermont's noted heroine, Ann Story. Story was one of the first settlers of Salisbury, Vermont. He said that he and his fellow pioneers could not have survived if it had not been for the wild animals. The pioneers had to be flesh eaters to survive. A few kinds of wild vegetable life were edible, but fish, birds, and quadrupeds were the indispensable and only food in the long winter months. The rivers, streams and lakes were literally "jumping with fish."

The famous Major Robert Rogers of the "Rangers" was invited by some friendly Indians to go salmon fishing with them one evening. They "filled a bark canoe with salmon in about half an hour." They used no hooks or nets; one Indian held a lighted pine torch to attract the fish to the side of the canoe where another Indian speared them. Dorothy Canfield Fisher tells of two young lads in Bennington County, Vermont, who caught a bushel-basketful of trout in an hour. Another writer reports that the Onion River "boiled with trout" in the good old days.

In Brownington, Vermont, four men caught "five hundred pounds of dressed trout in one day." A pond near a pioneer settlement was often called "our meat barrel," so full was it of fish. Fresh fish were nearly always to be had. Nor was it necessary to catch the fish in advance and preserve them by either smoking or salting them away, as they could be caught in the winter as well as the summer.

Fishing in the Connecticut River just below Bellows Falls and North Walpole was so good that settlers on both sides of the river neglected agriculture for many years. They fished not only for their own use but as a business to supply markets down river. The reason for this famous fishing hole was that the Great Falls in the river was a formidable obstacle for ocean fish to swim farther upstream to spawn. Salmon, with their fanatical persistence, managed to leap the falls and continue upstream to lay their eggs in the tributaries of the river. There was scarcely a river in New Hampshire or Vermont that emptied into the Connecticut or Lake Champlain or the Atlantic Ocean that was not good for salmon fishing during the spawning season in the old days when salmon weighing up to twenty pounds could be caught in large numbers. The Great Falls were, however, too much for the shad that also came up from salt water to spawn. Shad and their roe were prized by both Indians and whites who caught countless numbers to eat and sell down river after they were dried and smoked. Shad were so thick below the falls during the spawning season that "they could be caught by hand." Ocean salmon might still jump the original falls, but dams and filthy water long since put an end to a profitable business and a lot of fun.

Lake Champlain was full of lake trout, salmon, sturgeon and pike that were caught both summer and winter. And speckled trout were in every stream. The ocean coast of New Hampshire and Maine provided unlimited quantities of salt water fish, cod, salmon, halibut which weighed up to four hundred pounds, and clams, oysters, lobsters—but "since the growth of civilization, the oysters have disappeared from the whole coast between Nova Scotia and Cape Cod."

As the unpolluted waters jumped with fish, the forest teemed with birds and quadrupeds, some of which were dangerous to man and his domestic animals. However, the importance of most of the wild animals to the pioneers is shown in the earlier chapter on Seth Hubbell. There were wolves, moose, deer, bears, panthers or "catamounts," partridges as thick as barnyard hens, wild turkeys, pigeons, eagles, wild cats or lynx, beavers, muskrats, foxes, raccoons, porcupines, skunks, woodchucks, martens, rabbits, weasels, mink, otter, squirrels and many others. Nearly all of these in one way or another contributed to the food, clothing, floor and bed coverings of the pioneers. The hides often took the place of money at the trading posts and early stores.

The moose was the largest of the animals, sometimes

seven feet tall, weighing up to thirteen hundred pounds and with horns spreading eight feet from tip to tip. He satisfied his hunger with water plants, shrubs and moss and the bark of trees, especially the beech. The moose asked for nothing from the pioneers except to be left alone. This was seldom done, for his several hundred pounds of good meat was in great demand.

Deer were everywhere and became something of a pest when crops began to be grown. But they more than paid their way with venison and hides for clothing, shoes and hats, as in the "leather stocking" days immortalized by James Fenimore Cooper. Deer leather clothing was, in fact, worn by Davy Crockett when he was a member of Congress from Tennessee in 1827 and later.

Actually deer meat was so important that several Yankee towns at an early date voted an "off season" for deer hunting, and elected "deer reeves" as game wardens to protect them.

We now come to bears. A pioneer log cabin belonging to Thomas Davis in Grafton, Vermont, had an opening for a door, but no door, only an old bed quilt where the door was supposed to be. The wife pestered her husband for months to build a strong, solid door, but without result; he was too busy with more important work, he thought.

Later when the good wife was alone, knitting, and the cabin was filled with the fragrance of supper, a big bear poked his nose through the door. The wife screamed and probably threw hot water at the bear, which fled. All other operations ceased completely until a solid door filled the opening. Although bears were valuable for their flesh, grease and skins, the pioneers would probably have voted to do without them, and would surely have done so if woman suffrage had been permitted at town meetings. Bears destroyed growing corn and garden crops. They "relished" honey, calves and little pigs. An 1809 history of Vermont says, "There were instances in which children have been devoured by the bear, but it is only when it is much irritated, or suffering with hunger, that it makes any attack upon the human race." One night when her husband was away a Mrs. Graves of Brookfield, Vermont, heard loud noises in the pig pen and found a bear trying to get at their swine. She seized a pitchfork, climbed on top of the pig pen and thrust the fork at the bear whenever he got near the squealing pigs. She and the bear kept this up all night. Every pig was saved.

Wolves had no assets whatever. They were not valued for either flesh or fur, and they made it almost impossible to raise sheep. A small pack of wolves could destroy a flock of sheep in a single night, and even attacked men. From the beginning bounties were paid for killing them, and they were practically eradicated by the time pioneering ended.

The most feared wild animal was the panther or catamount. His "scream" made blood run cold. It was like that of a completely terrified woman. Actually the panther's "image" was worse than the animal. We are told in the *Field Guide to American Wild Life* that "there are no authentic records that this large, shy cat has ever made an unprovoked attack on a human being." But the pioneers in the Vermont and New Hampshire

A hungry bear.

wilderness in the late 1700s never read this book. Nor would they believe it if they had. The catamount was a powerful animal and as quick as lightning. In the Vermont Historical Society Museum at Montpelier there is a stuffed panther which was killed in Barnard, Vermont, in 1881. From nose to tip of tail it is seven feet, six inches long. Its girth is three feet, eight inches and its weight one hundred and eighty-two pounds. One old record tells us that a panther "took a large calf out of a pen, where the fence was four feet high, and carried it off. With this load it ascended a ledge of rock where one of its leaps was fifteen feet in height. After being shot and hit twice, its fury did not cease but with the last remains of life."

Prior to 1799 the Treasurer of Vermont had paid fifteen panther bounties at $10 each and six hundred wolf bounties at $20 each. This was big money in those days and shows how important it was to get rid of these beasts.

The panther's small cousin is the wildcat or Canadian lynx which weighs up to forty or fifty pounds. When one is alone in the woods at dusk, without a gun or even a stick, it is no fun to look a wildcat in the eye. I know; I did it once. Panthers and wildcats levied heavy tribute on the settlers' sheep, calves and pigs.

Of all the animals previously mentioned, probably the fiercest was the marten, closely related to the sable and fisher, with a body length up to thirty inches. It would tackle porcupines at sight and tear them to pieces. It is said that if two grown males meet, only one survives. Their fur, however, was very valuable, and Seth Hubbell counted it one of his few lucky days when he caught a marten or sable.

And now comes the most lovable wild animal of them all, then and now, the beaver. Without saw or axe, beavers gnaw down trees up to a foot in diameter. This is done in such a way that the trees nearly always fall where the beavers want them to. They then gnaw off the branches and cut the tree into logs of the right length for building their homes and dams. To have safe homes, the front door is under water and out of sight. They build dams to keep the water high enough to hide the entrance to their homes and also to provide easier transportation of the logs. In doing this, they create ponds and marshes which cover from one to a hundred acres or more.

In Williams's *History of Vermont* (1809) there is a charming description of the home life of these busy little citizens who peopled the wilderness long before the red or white men came. I quote briefly:

> In September, the happy couple lay up their store of provisions for winter. This consists of bark, the tender twigs of trees and various kinds of soft wood. When their provisions are prepared, the season of love and repose commences.
>
> During the winter they remain in their cabins, enjoying the fruits of their labor and partaking of the sweets of domestic happiness. . . . If any injury is done to their public works, the whole society are soon collected, and join all their forces to repair the injury which affects their commonwealth.

Nothing can exceed the peace and regularity which prevails in the families and throughout their commonwealth. No discord or contention ever appears in any of their families. There is no pilfering or robbing from one another. . . . Different societies of beavers never make war upon another, or upon any other animals.

What an example to mankind! No crimes, wars, divorces, beggars or drunks!

[21]

Passenger Pigeons

The old-time histories tell of the great flocks of pigeons that frequented the New England wilderness. But were they the famous "passenger pigeons" that covered the northeastern quarter of the United States from the Atlantic coast westward through the Abraham Lincoln country and beyond? It would seem so.

There were many other birds such as wild turkeys, geese and ducks, not to mention some of the songbirds of today. Flocks of pigeons, however, were so numerous as to "darken the sky" and break down the branches of trees from their sheer weight when they roosted at night. Acres of land under groves of beech trees were covered with their dung. Beechnuts, acorns and the catkins of birch and alder were their favorite foods, and their restless, long-distance flights in search of these, and nesting grounds, gave them the name "passenger pigeons." In the spring as they flew by the millions from the Florida Everglades as far north as Hudson Bay and Nova Scotia and west to Mississippi and beyond, they looked like a cloud of giant locusts circling in dark masses twenty miles wide. Early settlers wrote of pigeons' nesting grounds ten miles wide and eighty miles long, with every tree and bush laden with nests. The flocks did not stay long at one place, however, probably because they ate every edible thing in sight.

They were so destructive of growing crops on cleared land that they were destroyed by all available methods. It was impossible to grow wheat and other kinds of grain and berries in the presence of these huge flocks of birds. Audubon in 1842 saw a single flock outside of New England which he estimated to contain over one billion birds, and which he calculated covered an area one hundred and eighty miles long. He figured this one flock would eat eight million bushels of food in a single day. They were usually described as "voracious and greedy and the damage they did on cultivated land can scarcely be imagined." During the height of passenger pigeon migrations, farmers would stop work to kill them by the thousands as they passed overhead. But gunpowder was expensive and most hunters, especially those who supplied the markets where the squabs were in great demand, used nets and traps. Pigeons were of value, however, not only for food but for their feathers which made beds and pillows warm and comfortable. One bridal gift consisted of "125 pounds of feathers, 7 yards ticking, a warming pan, pot and kettle."

A full-grown male was a sleek and handsome bird, twenty inches tall, with a blue-gray back and a breast of robin red. The females were smaller, solid blue-gray and as graceful as doves with their long pointed tails

edged in white. Both had blood red eyes, strong black
bills and tiny red feet. In the Peabody Museum at Salem,
Massachusetts, there is a stuffed female passenger
pigeon and it is surprising to see what a beautiful bird
it was. It has been estimated that in the early 1800s,
forty per cent of the bird population in the United States
was passenger pigeons, and it seemed inconceivable that
they would ever disappear. Yet their wanton slaughter
over the years was such that within a hundred years the
last wild pigeon was killed. On March 24, 1900, a little
boy with a BB gun shot it in an oak grove in Pike
County, Ohio. One passenger pigeon which had been
trapped in 1885 was still living at that time in the Cin-
cinnati Zoological Gardens Zoo. The average life of a
passenger pigeon was less than ten years. But "old
Martha" lived to the incredible age of twenty-nine,
dying in 1914. It was almost as if, the last of her kind,
she refused to die.

[22]

Rattlesnakes

Among the seldom mentioned hazards of pioneer days were rattlesnakes. They were not too numerous in New England, but the known presence of a snake in a township was a fearful thing to contemplate, especially by women. Around Bennington, Vermont, rattlesnakes were so numerous that the first town meeting voted to pay a bounty for each snake killed. In some areas of Windsor County, Vermont, rattlesnakes were so thick that farm hands refused to go there to work. As one of them said, "I don't feel no call to tackle them."

An old folk song, too long to quote here in its entirety, put it:

> He scarce had twice mowed round the field
> When a pizen serpent bit his heel.

He died from the poison, and his sweetheart from grief.

Fall Mountain, opposite Bellows Falls on the Connecticut River, was a favorite habitat of the reptiles as they like rocky ridges with sunny exposures. They have gradually been killed off by men, by fires that swept over the mountain and by hogs which attacked and killed them at sight, being themselves protected by their tough hides and thick jowls in which snake's poison was so slowly absorbed as to do little harm. In New Hampshire there were several hills called "Rattlesnake Mountain." The *New Hampshire Gazetteer* of 1823 states that the towns of Raymond, Weare and Rumney, as well as Fall Mountain in Walpole, had these poisonous "varmints." It is probable that other towns did also, but were not inclined to boast about them. I have never seen or "heard tell" of a single live rattlesnake in New England during my lifetime.

Rattlesnakes were not entirely useless to the pioneers, however. Some of them valued "rattlesnake oil" for medicinal purposes. Indians used their skins as belts to hold up their loincloths.

[23]

The Same War—Insects

"We know only what we have lived," some wise man said. Few of the hardships which the pioneers faced in the 1600s and the 1700s confront us today. We are proud of the grit with which our ancestors faced the harsh environment of their times. But we cannot hear the howling of the wolves that they heard. The wolves are gone, and the twelve- and fifteen-hour day and the unending work. Only about seven per cent of our people still live on the land and work it. The rest have moved into the villages, towns and cities. They seem to have little in common with those who have gone before. But one enemy the pioneers fought we still have: insects. The experts say that insects have lived on this planet since the middle coal age, some three hundred million years before man arrived.

Today women may be more concerned about destructive insects than men. From time immemorial housewives have been battling insects of various kinds inside their homes—mosquitoes, flies, fleas, ants, cockroaches and bedbugs. Think what it was like when there were no such things as window or door screens, or even mosquito netting, much less the various death-dealing sprays now found in every supermarket. Millions of wives also have flower and vegetable gardens which they have to defend against insects. These trace back to the herb gardens of the first pioneers. There were no seed stores in the old days. Young wives going farther into the wilderness took packets of seeds, roots, or "slips" from their girlhood homes. They wanted a patch of garden that would give savor to food, medicine for the sick and nosegays for themselves.

Women today want the same things. Hence they carry on the same war against insects that was waged two centuries ago. Only the weapons have changed. The chinch bugs, ants, cut worms, termites, beetles, grubs and maggots that great-grandma fought are fought today. The lazy butterflies and the honey bees are about the only insects against which no war is fought. Veterans of different wars have much in common. But a stronger bond exists between veterans of the same war, a war that has had no end, no truce, since history began.

Let us turn now to the part that was played chiefly by the men and boys in the fields beyond the gardens. They could understand from personal experience the words in the Book of Exodus that "locusts covered the face of the earth . . . and there remained not any green thing." Thousands of insects are destructive of crops, fruit trees, farm animals and the health and life of men and women.

Yet the books on the old days in Yankee-land have

127

only a few pages on the lifelong struggle of the pioneers against destructive insects. The books are nearly as silent on destructive insects as they are on the one insect which is clearly on the plus side of civilization, the honey bee, concerning which we have devoted a chapter. Probably one reason there is so little mention of insects is that men said nothing because they could do little or nothing about them. In their stern philosophy "what can't be cured must be endured."

Over sixty years ago the U.S. Department of Agriculture wrote that insect losses in dollars were greater than all costs of education in all schools in the United States. Yet it is only recently that the Dutch elm disease and the writings of Rachel Carson have called general public attention to insects and insecticides.

To cut down an acre or two of primeval forest and let the sun shine on ground which had not felt its direct warmth for centuries; to "toe in" the first planting of the precious seed of corn or wheat and then watch the growing crop chewed up by insects against which they had no adequate defenses was a heartbreaking ordeal. The *General History of Connecticut 1781–1829* records that "caterpillars ate every green thing over a space of one hundred miles. The inhabitants of Verdmont [Vermont] would have perished of famine had not a remarkable providence filled the wilderness with wild pigeons. Three thousand people lived on the pigeons." (The pigeons also ate the insects.)

In 1770 Eleazer Wheelock of Hanover, New Hampshire, president of what is now Dartmouth College, wrote, "brown worms [caterpillars] four inches long attacked the crops; covered the ground—ten bushels of worms raked into a pile, blanketed the house inside and out." Timothy Dwight, ex-president of Yale College, wrote that grasshoppers in Bennington, Vermont, ate the silk off growing corn and killed the crop. He also recorded in his four-volume *Travels Through New England* in 1812 that the Hessian fly was a serious pest to growing wheat. And after the wheat was in the barn, it then had to face the weevils.

The larvae of the codling moth fed on apple and other fruit trees. In addition to grain, weevils infested nuts and the bark of trees. The gypsy moth, chinch bug, potato beetle, termite ants and many another insect ate their fill on what the settlers had worked twelve-hour days to raise. Other insects attached themselves to cattle, horses and sheep—parasites such as the screw worm, botfly, lice and fleas, always reducing the animals' vitality and in time killing them.

The common housefly is worldwide and was probably the worst offender of all. It breeds in barn manure and outdoor privies. As barns and barnyards were usually near the house, and sometimes under the same roof, flies polluted human food and helped spread anthrax, Asiatic cholera and the bubonic plague. Mosquitoes were largely responsible for typhoid fever and malaria. Then there were bedbugs, lice and ants. Even when insects did no direct harm to men or beasts, they exhausted their energy in fighting them off and in loss of sleep. Wire mesh to screen windows and doors was not invented until 1860. I have found no mention in any of the old books of "mosquito netting" or cloth screening.

Unless one covered his head with a blanket, the only partial protection from mosquitoes was smoke.

No wonder the pioneers welcomed the return of cold weather. Harvest time was the happiest season of the year, not only because husbands and wives and the children could see what they had accomplished, but because they could sleep soundly at night. The foregoing is not a pleasant tale, but it has to be told for us today to understand a little of what pioneer life really was, and the courage of those who lived it.

Despite the bugs and lack of insecticides, some splendid crops were grown in the rich leaf-mold where the forest had stood. But the leaf-mold does not get all the credit. I am indebted to entomologists for pointing out that in some instances it was the absence of particular insect pests at that location and point of time that permitted the crop to mature to its maximum yield. The bugs had not arrived.

The pioneers had other allies such as the insect-eating birds. Did you ever see a mother hen chasing a grasshopper with her little chicks running after her? Or a toad making a meal of insects? Or a trout leaping in a brook for a bug? There are dozens of species of fly-catching birds that live chiefly on insects, among which is the Red-eyed Vireo which was once the most abundant bird in North America. Modern insecticides, wisely used, have been a great blessing. But before they emerged from the laboratories, the age-old balance of nature often did yeoman work for the pioneers.

[24]

The Call of the Hills

In the hilly sections of New England most of the early
settlers chose their home sites on the high places instead
of in the valleys. Why? The reason often given today is
that they could see Indians approaching better than if
they were in the valleys, and also because Indians running uphill couldn't attack as easily. This was seldom
the real reason. When the land was all forest it would
have been hard to see Indians. The danger of Indian
attack was actually greater in the river settlements because the Indians often traveled by canoes. The chief
reason why the settlers chose the hills was that there
were more beaver than people in the long-ago days,
animals which had the inconsiderate habit of damming
up brooks and rivers until the lowlands were an impenetrable marsh. The swarms of mosquitoes, gnats,
blowflies and other insects that made life miserable for
man and beast were not quite so thick on the hills as in
the dank and swampy valleys choked with willows,
alders and brush.

It was believed that the chance of escaping malaria, typhoid fever and other crippling diseases was better on the drier hillsides. Moreover, there were more hours of sunlight on the hills and upland meadows for the growing of crops. The sun shone earlier in the morning and lingered later in the day on the eastern and southern slopes. In effect this lengthened the growing season by several days, an important consideration. And the season's first frosts hit the valley farms earlier and harder than the hill farms. In building a house or cabin, it was erected whenever possible so that the rooms most used faced east and south to catch the sunlight. This also helped to save firewood in the winter.

Another requirement of the home site was the nearness of a spring of pure water for the settlers and their animals, and these were often found on hillsides.

However, whether inadvertently or otherwise, the settlers found their own solution to the problem of swampy valleys by killing the ubiquitous beaver until the lowlands were drained and dried up. Roads that in the early days were little better than trails came down from the high ground where they had crept painfully over mountains and hills, and took to the valleys, often paralleling rivers and streams, and soon were followed by mills and taverns, blacksmith shops and homes. Proof that the beaver, only within recent years coming back into his own, was something to be reckoned with, lies in the fact that a tremendous fur trade existed in the early days along the Connecticut River. Furs were bundled and packed in hogsheads for shipment to England. In six years, John Pynchon of Springfield, Massachusetts, shipped forty-seven hogsheads of beaver alone, amounting to 8,992 skins, weighing 13,139 pounds. Otter, mink, muskrat, sable, fox and raccoon were sources of much revenue for the early settlers, who found most of New England a gold mine of fur. It was no wonder that, when the bogs and marshes dried up, many came down from the hills to the rich lands of the valleys. But many elected to stay on the hillsides. The upland farm had a "view." A view has meant much to people of all races and times. But it meant more to our Yankee forebears, for whom the days were never long enough to do the work that had to be done. They understood the Bible words, "I will lift up mine eyes to the hills from whence cometh my help."

[25]

Iron

Gold is for the mistress, silver for the maid,
Copper for the craftsman, cunning at his trade.
"Good" said the Baron, sitting in his hall,
"But Iron, cold Iron, is the master of them all."

—RUDYARD KIPLING

Despite the magnificence of New England's "endless forest," large sections were doomed to be cut down, not to keep the pioneers warm, or to grow their food, or to build houses, barns, bridges and fences, or as material for making potash. The reason was the need for iron. Iron is the fourth most abundant of the elements and comprises five per cent of the earth's crust. A little of it can probably be found in everyone's garden. During thousands of years, iron sometimes collects in the muck and sludge at the bottom of swamps and becomes "bog

134

iron ore." In the old days and for a short time, iron was smelted from the "magnetic sand" of the salt water beaches of Connecticut. However, iron ore in profitable quantity was generally associated with very hard rock such as granite.

The North American Indians, who had lived here ten thousand years or more, never had an Iron Age or a Bronze Age, both of which had been developed in the Old World for centuries. In the Old Testament iron implements are mentioned many times. It therefore seems quite incredible to us today that until the white men came to the New World, no North American Indian had ever seen a nail, pin, scissors, pot, hoe, saw or gun made of iron. Such things were so greatly desired by Indians that in 1638 a tribe sold the land that is now New Haven, Connecticut, and its environs to colonists from Massachusetts for twenty-four knives, twelve hatchets, twelve spoons, hoes, porringers, scissors and twenty-three coats. The iron articles must have been imported from England, as the famous Iron Works at Saugus, Massachusetts, was not yet in production. The American Iron and Steel Institute says "The American Indian never found the secret of the manufacture of iron."

Meteors or "falling stars" become very hot in passing through the atmosphere and sometimes contain bits of iron. With this exception, iron is very seldom found free from its surrounding ore or rock. The ore has to be melted to free the iron contained in it. This melting is done in a smelter where burning charcoal, aided by air (oxygen) from a bellows, develops heat enough to liquify both ore and iron, and thus separates the iron. The heat is about eleven times that of boiling water.

The red men knew how to make fire by friction but they had never learned that it was necessary to burn wood into charcoal that produces heat high enough to smelt metals from their ores. A wood fire burns at too low a temperature to do this. They never had a smelter. And so they continued to live in the Stone Age century after century. They had seen charcoal thousands of times in the ashes of their campfires, but never learned its secret.

In burning wood in your fireplace a piece of it often gets covered with ashes, but continues to burn slowly without bursting into flame. In the morning you have a small piece of black charcoal. It is almost pure carbon. If relighted, and made still hotter by air pumped into the fire by a bellows, you have the secret for obtaining heat hot enough to smelt iron.

In New England there were no huge deposits of iron ore, such as the Mesabi Range's, in the Lake Superior region, but there were many small ore deposits, close to the surface, such as bog ore as high as twenty-five per cent iron. These deposits often deflected the magnetic needle of the compass so as to cause errors by surveyors in laying out the boundaries of towns. The Europeans, as stated, had made iron for centuries. Hence within eight years after the landing at Plymouth Rock the pioneers looked for and found some bog iron ore deposits. The ore was assayed and in 1644, at Saugus, Massachusetts, they built the first successful iron smelter on the North American continent. It was one of the wonders of the age. They smelted some of the ore and produced, initially, enough iron to be cast into a small iron pot that would hold about a quart of water! The pot fortunately is still in existence and marks the birth of the most important single industry in America. The American Iron and Steel Industry has authentically rebuilt the pioneer "Works" at Saugus. It is a must to visit, a splendid tribute to the "spirit of enterprise" of the pioneers and of great historical significance. If it and other works like it had not been built, it is quite certain that the War of Independence could never have been won, or perhaps even started.

The British king and Parliament were glad to get raw materials including iron ore from the Colonies, but wanted to keep the manufacturing at home. At one time Parliament actually forbade the Colonies to make iron. An interesting sidelight on the Saugus Iron Works is that the works and all its employees were exempted from colonial taxes, military service or "watching for Indians." Soon smelters and blast furnaces dotted the New England landscape with Massachusetts in the lead for a long period, followed by Connecticut and Vermont. New Hampshire, Maine and Rhode Island also had some iron production. As many as a hundred iron works were in operation in New England at one time. Now, not one exists.

These "works" became beehives of industry to supply the raw materials of a rapidly growing country— plows, hoes, axes, cart tires, scythes, anvils, chains, ship anchors, stoves, spiders, kettles, etc. The men who burned wood into charcoal had the lonesomest, dirtiest and in many ways the most dangerous job in early New England. It was an expert occupation and apparently the men did little else except make charcoal. Cords of wood were stacked in mounds up to twenty feet in diameter and five or six feet high. The pile was then carefully covered with wet leaves, weeds and sod, with a small hole at the top as a sort of chimney. The fire had to be controlled to burn slowly without flame. In short, it was to do nothing but smoke for two weeks or more. The men had to stay on the job night and day, sleeping in miserable bark huts close to the burning mound. It was their responsibility to see that the wood never flamed. If it did, they had to put it out immediately by climbing on the mound and throwing wet sod or snow on it. Men sometimes fell into the burning wood and lost their lives. The charcoal burners were, and are, the forgotton men of the Iron Age. The historians have passed them by.

The demand for wood to make charcoal to smelt the iron created huge "cutovers" in the magnificent forests. As the production of iron increased, the demand for charcoal increased. Blacksmiths set up shop in every settlement and they also had to have charcoal to heat their iron. Many iron mines were abandoned, not because they had run out of ore, but because the forest had receded so far from the mine that the cost of bringing charcoal to the smelter became excessive. England and the Low Countries were nearly denuded of their once beautiful forests long before Plymouth Rock. According to Eric Sloane in his *American Heritage*, the small town of Salisbury, Connecticut, in 1840 was using five thou-

The need for iron.

sand cords of wood a year to make charcoal to smelt iron ore. As a cord is four feet high, four feet wide and eight feet long, this amount of wood, if laid in a single line, would be over seven miles long. In sections close to iron ore deposits, more wooded areas of land were cut down to make charcoal than were cleared to grow crops and to make potash as in the other sections of New England.

The land around Vergennes, Vermont, is an example. Before and during the War of 1812, it became the largest single iron-producing section in the United States. Vergennes for a short time boasted that it was the iron capital of the United States, with eight forges, a blast furnace and rolling mill. Here were built the ships with which Lieutenant MacDonough defeated the British fleet off Plattsburgh on Lake Champlain. "Hardly a mast was left standing in either fleet." Then the tide moved on to the West where America's huge deposits of coal and iron had been laid down long before either the red man or the white man came. They made coke in place of charcoal. In a few more years the iron industry of New England came to an end. Her forests could grow again.

It seems highly probable that the ability of the white men to make iron and steel axes, saws, plows, guns and scores of other metal tools and implements was the chief determining factor in the long struggle between the Indians and the whites for the mastery of the continent. Wood was used by the pioneers and their descendants to make dozens of useful articles, even wooden clocks, but it seems very doubtful that Europeans, women especially, would have come and stayed in this new land if they had nothing but stone and wooden implements, clam shells for spades and trowels, the shoulder blades of moose and deer for shovels and hoes for planting and weeding corn and pumpkins, and wooden tools for the fireplace. It may be said that if there had been no iron in America, the colonists would have imported iron implements from the old country. To some extent that is true. But the British forests had already been denuded to make charcoal and iron for home consumption. Freedom to worship God according to conscience is the principal reason given in many of the histories for our ancestors' sailing across the stormy North Atlantic, but American iron kept them from going back.

$\lceil 26 \rceil$

Isolation

Man is a gregarious animal and the loneliness of frontier life was a heavy cross to be borne. This was especially true of women. It made many women "queer" and some of them insane. But loneliness was seldom the sole cause of insecurity. Other factors were overwork, too many babies too close together, too many babies dying, in short, utter weariness of body and soul. There were many families with fifteen or more children. One of the first settlers in Whitingham, Vermont, in 1773, was a man named Pike. He had twenty-eight children, ten by his first wife and eighteen by two others. We may presume that his first two wives died. Most of his children lived to a mature age.

With only trails for roads and walking the only transportation, visits with relatives and friends were difficult and infrequent. Wives often entreated their husbands to move nearer to their relatives and friends, if only during the winter months. A few instances will illustrate how isolated the first-comers were:

The first settlers in Andover, Maine, were Ezekiel Merrill and wife in 1780. "His wife did not see another woman for three years." Abel Stockwell and Francis Whitmore lived in the same Vermont township of Marlboro for nearly a year before either knew of the presence of the other. Benjamin Copp was the first settler in Jackson, New Hampshire, in 1779, and "with his family buffeted the terrors of the wilderness for fourteen years before any other person settled there."

Hanover, New Hampshire, in 1762 had only two men. In Hillsborough, Mrs. James McCallen was the only woman in that town for a year. Deacon Aiken settled in Antrim in 1768. No other person moved into the town for the next four years. "He suffered much for want of friends and neighbors." Searsburg, Vermont, settled in 1791, had only nine inhabitants in 1820, twenty-nine years later.

In New England "town" is another name for "township." It is a geographical division of land, generally about thirty-six square miles. Isolation was bad enough on the grass-covered prairies of the Mississippi Valley, but there the sun could be seen and its warmth felt. Solitude was worse on the New England frontier which was almost entirely covered by an "unending" forest of trees, at the feet of which the sun did not penetrate until a clearing had been made. Many of the trees were evergreens that did not shed their leaves in winter.

However, it was only during the first year or two that a pioneer family had to endure the extreme gloom of the forest. A man could cut down one to three acres of trees in a season and let the sun shine on his cabin and patch of land. Many men did not fetch their wives into forest country until they had cleared several acres of land. But the forest was near in any case. Except for the cries of wild animals, the silence was profound, eerie, fear-inspiring. Men and boys on a rock ledge hilltop like to shout and wake the echoes, but in a forest men generally speak in low tones. Log cabins had tiny openings for windows, but no glass. Rooms were dim in daytime, except for fireplace light. A gloomy atmosphere has some connection with gloomy feelings. Women were indoors more than men.

Being alone in the wilderness had disadvantages other than the hunger to speak and to be heard. An isolated man or family had to do all the work necessary to keep alive, with only an occasional "lift" from a neighbor. Just to see, a mile across the valley, the smoke rising from the chimney of a neighbor meant much. Here was help if needed, whether a roof had to be raised or a baby born. Daniel Webster said of the term "the neighbors" that "nobody born in a city knows what the words mean." Except for occasional help from neighbors, it was self-help and self-reliance, a quality greatly valued until recent years. Ralph Waldo Emerson wrote a famous essay on the subject. When self-reliance goes, dependence on others begins. It is probable that this feeling of self-reliance, of personal independence, of going it alone, if necessary, which developed on the New England frontier in the century and a half after Plymouth Rock, had much to do with the Declaration of Independence in 1776.

When enough families "made their pitch" in the same

locality, it seems likely that the decision to build a church was whetted by the hunger to talk with one's neighbors as well as with God. Is it any wonder that they called it "The Meeting House"? Sabbath church-going meant sociability as well as sermons. It gave the women especially a time to talk.

From some three hundred or more books that I have read on this subject, it is not possible to learn all that the first-comers to wilderness country were up against. But there is a way to experience some of it. In Maine, New Hampshire and Vermont there are today twenty-two townships, each of which has less than one hundred inhabitants. This does not refer to hamlets or tiny villages within a township, but to the township itself with thirty-six square miles, more or less. You can find them on the automobile road maps. Drive to one of these tiny towns sometime and let its past come back. Spend a day or a week where others spent years. Visit it as you would visit a museum or battlefield or convention hall where men made history. These little towns made history. They are part of the dream of immigrant fore-fathers who crossed great waters "to be free and independent."

Lack of Medical Care

When some member of a pioneer family was seriously sick or hurt, nothing could measure their plight more truly than to say that skilled medical and surgical care was almost totally absent. There were very few doctors, and they were often miles from the man, woman or child who needed them. But it can be said unequivocally that the most highly regarded doctor in 1800, with thirty or forty years of active practice, would not now be permitted to practice medicine, surgery or dentistry in any state of the Union. He would not even be permitted to take the medical board examination because his application could not show that he had studied the required subjects in today's schools of medicine.

The first college of medicine was the Medical College of Philadelphia, established in 1765. Baltimore College of Dental Surgery, founded in 1839, was the first institution of its kind in the world. It was not until 1843 that the University of Pennsylvania gave the first course on obstetrics or "mid-wifery." With what little the students learned in the few early schools in America, none would be admitted to practice today.

"Bleed, puke and purge" was standard practice in the old days. In his last illness on December 12 to 14, 1799, George Washington had, no doubt, the ablest doctors available. He was "bled heavily four times, given gargles of molasses, butter and vinegar, and a blister of cantharides [ground up Spanish flies] was placed on his throat." (Spanish flies were also known as blister-beetles.)

Washington had come down with quinsy or acute laryngitis after an exhausting trip on horseback in cold and snow. Modern doctors would no doubt try to ease his throat, but not with dead beetles. Bleeding is very seldom done today for any reason. General Washington could not have been taken to any hospital. There were only two so-called hospitals in the United States, at Philadelphia and New York, two and five days from Mount Vernon by horseback or carriage.

Hundreds of Yankee pioneers, men, women and children, had no doubt the same sickness as Washington, with the same result. They had no hospitals, no ambulances, no paved highways, no drug stores, no trained nurses, and no life insurance or social security payable to a widow when her husband died. A widow was almost compelled to remarry to have someone to carry on and help bring up her children. Pregnant wives, for reasons of modesty, seldom saw a doctor even if there were one close enough to be consulted. There were no telephones. The doctor had to be sent for and found. And if he was not at home, but attending some other patient, finding him was a time-consuming job.

Young men who wanted to become doctors worked as apprentices to older men and learned what they knew. Some were self-taught. A tradition in a Vermont family which has produced four generations of doctors and nurses tells how the first doctor ancestor began his practice. Coming to his pioneer home in Vermont in 1801, he learned from experience how to doctor his own family through the use of home remedies concocted from bark, roots and herbs. Friendly Indians had taught him that the inner bark of the red elm, commonly called "slippery elm," if dried and reduced to powder, then made into a drink with the addition of sugar and water, was the best cure for sore throat, dysentery, diarrhea and even for nourishment in times of want. As recorded in his diary, he decided that he must be "skillful in whatever he set his hand to do," and after much deliberation he and his wife took twenty of their hard-earned dollars from their potash fund and invested in a book called *The First Right of Preparing and Using the System of Medical Practice*, edited by a Dr. Samuel Thomson, a New England botanic physician. With the book came his certification to practice medicine, and until his death in 1843 he administered to ailing townspeople at any time of the day or night. This method of learning was undoubtedly used by many devoted men in pioneer back-country who had no other way of acquiring the knowledge so sorely needed. There were many quacks who pretended to be doctors and took a cruel advantage of the ignorant. Even as late as the 1870s advertisements appeared in Vermont and New Hampshire such as: "Cancer can be cured positively by Dr. X., or your money back. See me at once."

On the other hand, most of the old-time doctors were dedicated men, and did the best they could. They were aware of how little they knew, and from the earliest days sought a better knowledge of how to cure the sick, or those crushed by a falling tree (a frequent accident), or gored by a bull, or cut by a flying axe. Small children often fell into the fireplace and were badly burned. That doctors were doing the best they could acted as a psychic balm on sick folks and their families. Few ever failed to go where sickness or accident called them because the family was poor. They took their pay in firewood, potash, potatoes, hay or whatever was offered them. Many never billed poor families and died poor themselves. They were friends as well as doctors. When the old-time doctor went to a lonely cabin, where sickness and fear prevailed, everyone felt better. When the doctor himself died he was greatly mourned.

From the earliest days these men sought to advance their medical knowledge. Statewide medical societies were formed in Vermont in 1784 and in New Hampshire in 1791. A medical school was established at Dartmouth College in 1797, one of the oldest in the United States. Massachusetts, however, of all the New England states, was the first to establish a medical school at Harvard in 1782. Yale, at New Haven, Connecticut, followed with its medical school in 1813. The Medical Department of the University of Vermont was established in 1804 with lectures on "chirurgery," an old-fashioned word for surgery. At Castleton, Vermont, a medical college was established in 1818, with lectures on anatomy the main course. Where they got the cadavers they studied aroused much curiosity.

Despite this search for medical truth, practically nothing was known about germs or bacteria as the chief cause of deadly diseases and their spread. Antiseptics, other than hot water, sunlight and rum were an undiscovered country. Decades were to pass before Jenner, Lister, Pasteur, Lock, Semmelweiss, Fleming and other giants of medical science discovered modern antiseptics and antibiotics. It was not until World War II that penicillin came into general use. The suffering that human beings endured for ages before reliable anaesthetics came into use can scarcely be imagined today. Generally, anything that cuts off or reduces the flow of blood and oxygen to the brain is a sort of anaesthetic. Numbness from cold is an example. All sorts of crude methods had been used by mankind to reduce pain. Getting a patient drunk before cutting off his leg was one. All such methods, of course, had serious disadvantages. It was not until 1842 that Dr. William Morton of Boston, a dentist, demonstrated the use of ether to reduce pain or produce general unconsciousness. Mankind had to wait until 1847 before a general anaesthetic was used successfully in childbirth. The pioneer mothers of New England were all in their graves by then.

The foregoing, however, is only part of the story. There was another doctor in the neighborhood, Mother Nature. Her remedies were clean air, sunlight, work, sweat and the pride of free men in visible accomplishments by the use of their hands and skills. The first settlers were a tough lot. Vermont's noted historian, Samuel Williams, writing in 1809, said of the pioneer, "Can their health and spirits remain unimpaired amidst this scene of hard labor and hard living? . . . No difficulty or hardship seemed to discourage them . . . the disorders which wear away the inhabitants of wealthy cities are almost unknown in the woods . . . the benevolent author of Nature has annexed to their health . . . temperance, industry, and activity which is never found in drugs or medicine."

The men who made the first settlements were a hardy group. "It is only those who are of the enterprising spirit who venture to try their fortunes in the woods," as Samuel Williams said. These men thrived on hard work. But mothers in childbirth and small children who died like flies in contagious epidemics needed modern medical care. Their mute gravestones in old cemeteries testify to this.

[28]

Home Remedies

In the absence of doctors, the pioneers used various remedies and nostrums, most of which seem fantastic to us. They fought death with all weapons, however foolish they seem to us. "Drowning men clutch at straws." Many of their cures gained credit because sick folks often survived both the sickness and the remedy. But in such cases the remedy got the credit. Then, too, many old-time herbs did have value. What were once the plants in a frontier woman's herb garden became, in some cases, the foundation of acknowledged worth in modern medicine. For example, deadly nightshade and foxglove have blossomed out today as belladonna and digitalis. One old-time remedy for a bleeding cut was spider webs. They hastened the coagulation of blood. Another remedy for cuts and wounds was mouldy bread. Penicillin comes from a mould.

Some very deadly diseases are cured without much "book larnin." Scurvy is scarcely heard of today, but in Yankee-land it was a deadly disease a hundred and fifty years ago, and later. In the Civil War fifteen per cent of all soldier deaths not caused by battle wounds were caused by scurvy. In the days of long voyages on sailing ships, members of the crew who had nothing but a diet of sea biscuits and salt meat were very apt to come down with scurvy. A simple cure turned up, lemons or limes! British sailors used to be called "Limeys" as a result of drinking lime juice which contains ascorbic acid, or vitamin C. Another remedy of the utmost importance was sunlight. Factory, mine and office workers today work in the shade with artificial light. Yet it has been known for centuries that death comes most frequently in January, February and March, when the hours of sunlight are the shortest.

Let us look at the materia medica of our ancestors:

Roasted porcupine juice dropped in the ears would cure deafness.

The gummy inner bark of slippery elm, mixed with gunpowder, was used as a poultice for rattlesnake bite.

Potato bugs, killed in vinegar and dried in the sun, were good for blisters.

A horse chestnut carried in the pocket would cure and prevent rheumatism.

Warts—pierce with a red hot needle.

A diet of skunk cabbage would cure asthma.

A drink of vinegar was a sure cure for fainting.

Human urine, as a disinfectant for cuts and wounds, "has saved many a life."

"To cure a belly ache, spit under a stone." This made one stoop and brought up the gas.

Shoes placed under a bed, soles up, would prevent nightmares.

Dock leaf, cooked into a poultice, was "a sure cure for cancer."

A powder made from chickweed was also "a sure cure for cancer."

For consumption, "inhale the smoke of burning mullein leaves."

For a cold, take very hot boneset, or pennyroyal, or catnip tea. This was also good for anyone feeling "tuckered out." Poplar bark steeped in water and taken frequently was another good tonic.

To keep colds from "going down," tie a stocking with salt pork and onions around the neck.

For whooping cough and measles, take a mixture of honey and lobelia. Another good remedy is to steep a white hornet's nest into a tea and drink it constantly.

Dried prickly ash berries mixed with rum produced a liquid fire good for "ague."

Wild turnips dried, grated and mixed with molasses were good for a hacking cough.

Skunk oil, both swallowed and rubbed on the chest, was good for croup.

For asthma, put a pint of angle worms into a bowl, add brown sugar and let it set until the worms are dead, then drink.

Dried eelskin tied around the affected limb was good for rheumatism.

To stop consumption from killing the entire family, bury the first victim face down.

Whiskey was used for fevers. Also for colds. Considered very effective.

Eat an apple 'fore going to bed and you'll make the doctor beg for his bread.

When Dr. John Arms, of Brattleboro, Vermont, was himself sick, he said, "I live on cornmeal pudding until my disease gets disgusted and leaves me."

$$\begin{bmatrix} 29 \end{bmatrix}$$

Accidents

A pioneer immigrant from Scotland wrote his father and mother in the old country, "My little boy which has Been very unwill these two months he fell in the fire and Burnt one part of his Head."

Fireplaces were on the same level as the cabin floor and required constant watching to keep toddlers and tottering old folks from stumbling into the fire. In those days there were no metal screens to put in front of the fireplace. Sparks were a constant hazard not only to people but to the building itself. They came from both the fireplace and the chimney and sometimes set the roof afire. Flues often became lined with creosote or wood-tar from the smoke of burning wood. This caused chimney fires which spread to the roof and then to the building itself. When cabins burned to the ground, the ashes were carefully raked to salvage any nails so they could be used again. Except for the nails, a burned cabin was a total loss. There were no fire insurance companies in New England until the early 1800s and then only in the larger communities where volunteer bucket brigades helped to put out fires. The pioneers' isolated homes and barns were lucky to escape destruction by fire.

Felling trees was always hazardous even to an expert axe-man. A falling tree was apt to bounce sidewards or kick backwards in unexpected directions when it hit the ground. The husband of the famous Ann Story was one of many who were killed by falling trees.

The father of Robert Rogers, of Rogers' Rangers fame, was mistaken for a bear and was shot and killed. He probably was wearing a greatcoat and hat made of bearskin, which was customary in those days, but dangerous. A four-year-old boy was killed by drinking lye that had been leached from wood ashes. The son of General Wait of Waitsfield, Vermont, was bitten by a mad dog. The nearest doctor was at Woodstock, forty-four miles away. Rabies or hydrophobia was a terrible hazard in pioneer days as it infected not only dogs but foxes, wolves, skunks and even deer and cattle. The wound from a mad animal's bite was burned by a hot iron, and if this was done quickly enough there was a good chance of avoiding a terrible death. Then there were broken bones, frozen feet, axe cuts, goring by bulls, snake bites, bee stings, drownings and many other accidents. Ethan Allen's brother Ira, and another man, were felling trees on the Onion River in Vermont, when the man cut his leg to the bone. Allen applied a poultice made from beech tree leaves and the bark of basswood roots. A complete recovery was reported. And nowhere in pioneer country was there such a thing as a completely sterile bandage or a bottle of iodine.

$\begin{bmatrix} 30 \end{bmatrix}$

Longevity

*Go sometimes to their graves and give an hour
of a summer's evening to the brave and pious dead.*
—RUFUS CHOATE

Because the matter of longevity is so interesting and
important in comparing the America of the 1700s with
the last half of our twentieth century, let us consider
what the gravestones have to say. Every gravestone is
a small history. It records at least the main events, birth,
marriage, and death. If the dead person had fought for
his country, that fact is also carved on stone.

Because the data on the stone were not put down by
strangers but by members of the immediate family who
knew the deceased well and had no reason to state anything but the truth, they are generally accepted by the
courts as facts. They are more reliable than town and
state histories, perhaps written at a time long after the
event. I have compiled the age at death of the Revolutionary War veterans who settled in Springfield, Ver-

mont, and are buried in its cemeteries. (Two of these veterans are my ancestors.) In a few cases, the age of the veteran was not known, but forty-six of them are recorded. Only one veteran died before the age of fifty and is omitted from this calculation. Only eight of the remaining forty-five died before they were seventy years old. One was ninety; seventeen were in their eighties, and nineteen in their seventies.

I also examined the records of the Revolutionary War veterans who are buried in Brandon, Vermont, and whose age at death is stated. For the towns of Springfield and Brandon combined, there were eighty veterans who lived beyond fifty years. The average age at death of these eighty men was 75.71 years. In short, when these eighty men were fifty years of age, they had a "life expectancy" of 25.71 years. The surprising fact is that these eighty Revolutionary War veterans lived a little longer than the average man of fifty is expected to live today.

These Revolutionary War veterans who settled in Springfield and Brandon, Vermont, came from all over New England. Very few, if any, were born in Vermont. It is probable too, that these New England Yankees who went to war in '76 were tougher than average to begin with, and probably above the general average of all men in their age group. Nevertheless, these facts should be of great interest to life insurance actuaries and to medical men who specialize in the diseases of old age, and in increasing the health and life span of the present and future generations. If a study were made of the age at death of eight thousand Revolutionary War veterans, rather than eighty, some surprising facts might emerge. The tremendous gains made by medical science in extending the average life span have been achieved primarily in saving the lives of babies, their mothers, young children and young adults. Medical science is of course a prime factor in the "population explosion" which is the other side of the coin.

The earliest American mortality table known to me is the "American Experience" table covering the years 1843–58. This is more than fifty years after the first permanent settlements of most Vermont and New Hampshire towns. Nevertheless, it covers a period when many of the early settlers were dying, or had recently died. This table shows that the average life expectancy of a newborn babe in 1843–58 was then 41.45 years. Compare that with the recent "Commissioners 1958 Standard Ordinary Table" for 1950–54. It shows the life expectancy of a newborn babe to be 68.30 years, a gain of 26.85 years over that of a child at the time of the 1843 table. This is one of the greatest achievements in all recorded history.

Now let us compare the expectancy of fifty-year-old men then and now. The early table of 1843 gives their expectancy at age fifty to be 20.91 more years of life. The later "Commissioners" table of 1958 gives the life expectancy of the average fifty-year-old man to be 23.63 years. This is a gain of only 2.72 years as against the gain during the same period of a newborn babe of 26.85 years. A noted newspaper columnist on health, Dr. George W. Crane, writes me that "people at the age of sixty are living on the average only about six to eight

Hardy, long-lived Revolutionary War veterans.

weeks longer than the sixty year olds in Abraham Lincoln's time." That is a gain of only about two months in the past one hundred years.

Why? It is my belief that the old-timers who survived the diseases of childhood, motherhood and young adult-hood without the aid of modern medical science, lived in an environment only slightly less favorable to long life than it is today. In short, the "good old days," at least for those who reached middle age, were not so bad after all.

These Revolutionary War veterans had no hospitals, no modern medical, surgical, or dental care. No trained nurses. Modern antiseptics, anaesthesia, antibiotics and vitamins were unknown. There was no international quarantine of infectious diseases. The old-timers faced pestilence, consumption, malaria, smallpox, scurvy, spotted fever, cholera and blood poisoning from cuts and accidents. They had no window or door screens, no rubber coats or boots, little or no refrigeration, no central heating or air conditioning. Insects, including the malaria mosquito, swarmed over them and their food day and night. Probably a majority, including the women, went barefoot six months in the year, from "frost to frost." They were cold in winter, hot in sum-mer, wet in slush and rain. They worked seventy to eighty hours a week. They had few days off and no vacations as we know them. Yet without our modern aids to health and comfort, the New England pioneers changed a wilderness into a civilization in twenty or thirty years after the first settlements. How were these veteran soldiers and their neighbors able to do so much despite their handicaps? One answer is that most of them had elbow grease and the sparkplug of ambition. They were not afraid of work. They were afraid of debt. They had read the Bible and the command from above, "In the sweat of thy face shalt thou eat bread," not the sweat of others. They did not think they had committed a social sin if their faces and clothes were drenched in sweat. Work did them good and hardship made them tough. Only from struggle comes strength. As Vermont's first historian, Samuel Williams, wrote in 1809, "Temperance and labor do more for them than art and medicine can do for others."

The fifty-year-old men and women of today, in contrast to their ancestors, are generally soft and fat. A majority are overweight. They eat too much, drink too much, smoke too much, don't walk enough and drive too fast. Fifty thousand are killed every year on the highways, one every eleven minutes, and there is one highway injury every eighteen seconds.

Millions of people now breathe polluted air and drink polluted water made potable only with chlorine or other chemicals. They seldom, if ever, smack their lips over a drink of cool sweet water bubbling from a hillside spring. Their working hours are short, but most of them work indoors under artificial light and under almost constant noise and tension. When not at work, they are seldom free from the noise of screeching brakes, honking horns and the insults of seventy- or eighty-mile-per-hour drivers. This goes by the name of "progress." They swallow billions of pills to calm their nerves, put them to sleep and wake them up.

The pioneers worked from sunrise to moon-up, but they went at a slower pace. Their oxen and horses walked only four or five miles an hour. No speed laws were needed. After the forests were cleared, the men spent most of their days in the sunlight and clean fresh air. The women also spent much of the summer working in the sunlight, hanging out the wash and tending the gardens. The noises they heard were mostly the baas of sheep, the moos of cows, the whinny of the old mare, the hum of bees and the music of birdsong.

It seems plain that for those who have reached the half-century mark, the potential benefits of twentieth century medicine and science to health and happiness are being largely canceled out by the environment and personal habits this century has created.

Information, Please gives the following figures on life expectancy for white males in the United States:

In 1850, at age fifty, men had a life expectancy of 21.6 years; in 1964 the figure was 23.2 years, a gain of 1.6 years. Sixty-year-old men in 1850 had an expectancy of 15.6 years. In 1964, their expectancy was only 16 years, a gain of four-tenths of a year, or a little more-than four months in one hundred and fourteen years.

An article on "Longevity" in the *Encyclopedia Americana* states: "Only a complete revolution in our mode of life, involving a return to the slow, quiet life of the country, plus the advantages of modern medical science gives any hope for an increase in human longevity."

The *Encyclopedia Britannica* says: "Retirement, often looked forward to in early life, is a source of danger as it may well bring with it cessation of activity," and

164

"Poverty, within limits, is an advantage as it removes the danger of excessive eating, particularly of meat, after the body has reached maturity."

The famous Dr. Paul Dudley White writes that coronary heat disease "has become epidemic."

Dr. Wilhelm Raab, cardiovascular research director at the University of Vermont College of Medicine, says that "Lack of exercise is the major cause of coronary heart disease." Nearly every tool or implement for sale today is advertised as "labor saving" as its great incentive for purchase. The movement of tens of millions of our people from the land into the crowded Babylons which we call cities must certainly be a factor in the conditions which brought about the above observations. An internationally respected authority, Dr. René Dubos, asks, "Can man survive life in big cities?"

As a layman, I can only answer by citing an old Greek legend. Hercules was the strongest man in the world, but Antaeus was the world's undefeated champion wrestler. The two men were matched. Hercules consulted an oracle to find out the secret of Antaeus. He was told that as long as Antaeus could touch the earth with foot, knee, hand or shoulder, he drew invincible strength from the earth. When the two giants met, Hercules lifted his opponent from the earth and crushed him to death.

[31]

Giants in the Earth

One of humanity's best traits is the pride that men and women take in feats of strength, endurance and great age of their ancestors. No doubt this leads to some exaggeration that does not please the strictly scientific mind. But if so, it is more comfortable to think that we come from giants rather than pygmies.

There were giants in the earth in those days—mighty men which were of old. (Genesis 6:4)

What follows are records to be found in the old books, chiefly about the length of life of our Yankee ancestors in the 1700s. Palfrey's *History of New England*, which was published in the year 1866, says that "if the official returns of deaths in Massachusetts for four consecutive years may be credited, one person in every eighteen then living was more than eighty years old." This is a ratio of 5.5 per cent. The Institute of Life Insurance in New York City advises me that today only 1.5 per cent of our people are eighty or more. This is fifteen in one thousand. Stated otherwise, nine hundred and eighty-five Americans in a thousand now die before they are eighty years old.

The New Hampshire Historical Society reported in 1827 that between 1686 and 1826, or one hundred and forty years, three hundred and thirty-six of the state's citizens had lived to be ninety years old or more, and that ninety-two lived to be one hundred or more. The oldest, Zacchaeus Lovewell, of Dunstable, lived to be one hundred and twenty. William Perkins, of Newmarket, died at the age of one hundred and sixteen. That was in 1732, the year George Washington was born.

In Salem, New Hampshire, where my great-grandfather Peter was born in 1769, "Abiel Austin who behaved gallantly at the battle of Pigwacket" in 1724, lived to be eighty-six. The first settlers in Londonderry, lived an average of eighty years. Hollis, for the years 1775–1820, reported that one in nine of its inhabitants had lived to be eighty or more.

The classic story of longevity is that of George Gardner of Pownal, Vermont, who came from Hancock, Massachusetts, in 1765. Most of the early settlers were young men and women. But Gardner was eighty-five when he came. One of the first things he did was to plant apple seeds in his clearing. No doubt he got a lot of "ribbing" from his young neighbors who wanted to know why a man eighty-five years old was planting apple seeds. We can imagine his reply: "So that I will have apples to eat when I get old. I like apples and cider and apple jack." He lived to be one hundred and fourteen years old and ate apples from his own trees.

The *New Hampshire Gazetteer* published in 1823 states that "The healthiness of the state . . . may be estimated from the great number of instances of longevity which it has furnished." Names are given of seventy-six centenarians of whom six were living in 1823. The pioneers were proud of their many instances of sturdy long life. Claims were made by townships and even states (as by real estate promoters today) that they were unusually healthy places to live in; for example, "Resinous forest trees produce a balsamic quality to the air which is very favorable to good health." Such was the claim of New Hampshire's noted historian, Jeremy Belknap.

In short, there seems to have been a sort of rivalry among the different communities as to which has the better climate and the more old folks in proportion to population. It is doubtful that there was deliberate falsification, but whatever doubts arose were almost sure to be resolved on the "up" side. Old people who were born elsewhere did not always have the family Bible or church records telling when they were born. This was more often the case with respect to those born in "foreign parts."

There was also a natural self-selection of physical fitness for pioneering in new country. The ones who stayed behind in established villages in Rhode Island, Massachusetts and Connecticut included many who were physically unable or too timid to start a new life in the deep forest farther on.

Many of these old-timers were remarkably vigorous. Mrs. Lyman Stiles, of Somersworth, New Hampshire, walked two miles to church and back until she was ninety, and then lived eleven more years. Robert Macklin of Wakefield, New Hampshire, a native of Scotland, frequently walked from Portsmouth to Boston, or sixty-six miles, in one day, and returned on foot the next day. He did this for the last time in his eightieth year. Because this seemed to me, as it may to you, to be either a "tall story" or a printer's error, I found that the world's record for walking thirty miles is four hours and three minutes.* This indicates that sixty-six miles in a day was not impossible for Mr. Macklin, however much it would be for us. They were giants in those days.

* *Encyclopedia Britannica* 1966 Year Book.

[32]

Death and Burial

Under the most bearable circumstances death and burial are a sad business. Today, however, most of the necessary details are handled by professional undertakers who are not emotionally involved. The grave is not dug by members of the family.

In the old days, in winter when the ground was frozen solid, it was almost impossible to dig a grave with the few poor tools available to a frontier family. Even today there are few winter burials in northern New England. The dead body is kept in a vault until spring, when it is interred in a grave with appropriate ceremony and prayers. But death came also to isolated frontier families in the depth of winter, when the ground was frozen hard and snow was deep. Many times there were no boards or planks to make a coffin because there was no sawmill within reach. What then?

The first person to die in Cambridge, Vermont, was

170

buried in a trough cut from a basswood log. In Wilton, New Hampshire, a Mr. Badger died and "there being no boards, a pine tree was cut down and a trough dug out of it for a coffin; a piece was hewed for a cover and in this manner he was buried." In this instance "buried" indicates that a grave was dug; that the ground was not frozen.

In a Vermont wilderness a wife died in the middle of winter. Her husband also had no boards with which to make a rude coffin. How could he keep her body safe from wolves and bears until spring? He put his wife's body in a fallen hollow tree and plugged the open end of the tree with big stones to foil the wild beasts until spring came when he could dig her grave. This is the most poignant incident of pioneer history that I have read. In Tamworth, New Hampshire, in the late fall, a husband knowing that his sick wife could live but a few weeks longer, dug her grave while she was still alive, and before the ground froze. When a deadly epidemic swept through a family, killing two or even three children, it was not unusual to bury two or more bodies in the same grave.

In a grave in Grafton, Vermont, marked by a famous double headstone, lie the bodies of a young son and thirteen infants, together with the mother who died in 1803. As far as I know, this is the record number of bodies in one grave. Apparently each infant was born dead, and they were buried one after the other in the same grave. The inscriptions on the double stone read as follows:

IN MEMORY OF
THOMAS K. PARK, JUN.
AND THIRTEEN INFANTS
CHILDREN OF
MR. THOMAS K. PARK
AND REBECCA HIS WIFE

Youth behold and
shed a tear
See fourteen children
slumber here
See their image how
they shine
Like flowers of a fruit-
ful vine

IN MEMORY OF MRS.
REBECCA PARK, WIFE OF
MR. THOMAS K. PARK
WHO DIED SEPT. 23
1803 IN THE 40TH YEAR
OF HER AGE

Behold and see as you
pass by
My fourteen children
with me lie
Old and young you soon
must die
And turn to dust as well
as I

Rubbing, Park family gravestone.

Upon a gravestone in an old cemetery in Hartford, Connecticut, these words are inscribed:

> They fell like young oaks which stood alone on the hill. The traveler saw the lonely trees and wondered how they grew so lovely. The blast of the desert came by night and laid their green heads low. Next day he returned, but they were withered and the heath was bare.

Pioneer life was often very grim. Before the white men came, and after they came, the red men used the bark of elms and other big trees to cover their dead in shallow graves. In the absence of anything better, the white men often did the same. When graves were dug and an old person was buried, a sheaf of golden grain was often laid on the grave, a symbol of days and the gathered harvest. Sometimes the sheaf was later carved on the stone.

[33]

Patterns

George Niles of Shaftsbury, Vermont, lived to be one hundred and five years old. On his hundredth birthday, which came in haying time, his sons, together with their sons, daughters, wives and neighbors came from miles around to do the old man honor. He called his sons "boys," although they were grown men, fifty, sixty, or seventy years old, and experienced farmers themselves. Tradition tells, in substance, how he responded to their good wishes:

"Boys, fetch me a scythe," he said. So they fetched him a scythe.

"Is she whetted good?" the old man asked.

"Just off the grindstone, father. You could shave with it."

The old man took the scythe and felt its razor edge with his thumb. Satisfied, he took the scythe in the crook of his arm and walked out in the meadow where there was a beautiful stand of timothy, or "herd's-grass," as the old-timers called it.

The "boys" followed. And all the neighbors, men and women, children and dogs. The old man had swung a scythe in that meadow for fifty years or more. No one said a word.

The centenarian began to mow. With each swing of the scythe he caught the falling grass on the "heel" of his scythe and deposited it in a beautiful windrow at his left. After going thirty feet or so he stopped. His swath was as straight as a drawn string, every blade of grass cut neat and trim. He was breathing sweet and easy.

"Look thar, boys," he said, "Thar's a pattern for ye!"